The Next Left

The Next Left

THE HISTORY OF A FUTURE

Michael Harrington

An Owl Book

HENRY HOLT AND COMPANY

New York

Copyright © 1986 by Michael Harrington
All rights reserved, including the right to reproduce this
book or portions thereof in any form.
Published by Henry Holt and Company, Inc.,
115 West 18th Street, New York, New York 10011.
Published in Canada by Fitzhenry & Whiteside Limited,
195 Allstate Parkway, Markham, Ontario L3R 4T8.

Library of Congress Cataloging-in-Publication Data
Harrington, Michael, 1928–
The next left.
Bibliography: p.
1. Socialism. 2. Capitalism. 3. United States—
Economic policy. 4. United States—Social policy.
I. Title.
HX73.H369   1987   338.973   86-18446
ISBN 0-8050-0104-2
ISBN 0-8050-0792-X (An Owl book: pbk.)

First published in hardcover by Henry Holt and Company, Inc.,
in 1987.
First Owl Book Edition—1988

Designed by Lucy Albanese
Printed in the United States of America
1 3 5 7 9 10 8 6 4 2

ISBN 0-8050-0792-X

Contents

Acknowledgments

I am indebted to the students in my seminars at Queens College and the Graduate Center of the City University of New York who helped me work out some of these ideas.

The chapter on France grew out of the Gaus Seminars at Princeton University in 1984 as well as from my teaching at the Paris-VIII (St. Denis, formerly Vincennes) campus of the University of Paris in the Spring of 1983.

My participation in the work of the Socialist International during the period of research and writing gave me the opportunity to discuss some of these ideas with the leaders of the European democratic Left.

The members and friends of Democratic Socialists of America, activists committed to making the values of this book real, were some of my best teachers.

Finally, this volume is dedicated to Dick Seaver, not simply a fine editor, but an extraordinarily decent man who contracted for this book with a cancer patient. May it vindicate his humanity.

The Next Left

1

The Next Left

The Western Left will confront the possibility of political power within the next five years, and perhaps sooner rather than later.

No one knows when or for what immediate reasons that possibility will manifest itself. But it will come. Only that in no way guarantees that the next Left will successfully respond to the opening. It may well be overwhelmed by the very events that give it a new chance; it may simply lack the creativity to deal with a crisis that has already bankrupted so much of American liberal and European socialist ideology.

I write to forestall such a failure and, in some small way, to help the next Left seize its coming opportunity.

What has just been said might seem to be preposterous in the mid-eighties. After all, the Western Left—and I write primarily about Europe and North America—lives in the shadow of François Mitterrand and Ronald Reagan, of abject socialist failure and obvious conservative success. How can one possibly argue under these conditions that the Left must now prepare itself for the dangers of power?

1

In 1981, François Mitterrand and his party achieved a political dominance unheard of in France even under Charles de Gaulle. With a strong presidency and a majority in the National Assembly, they proceeded to put their entire program into effect. And yet within one year they were in retreat and within two in a rout. If one then counters that the Spanish and Swedish Socialists are in much better political shape after their recent years in office, it has to be at least noted that they pursued what seem to be rigorously capitalist policies. That may be a tribute to their realism, but not to their proclaimed political philosophy.

At the same time, President Reagan did indeed set off a deep recession in 1981–82, but then he presided over a strong recovery that lasted into the middle of 1984. So he campaigned in triumph for a second term and even stole the Democrats' political clothes in the process—the claim that the party of Franklin Roosevelt could, of course, manage the economy better than the Republicans. Ironically, we now know that at the very moment that Reagan was convincing a majority of the people that he had created the conditions for a new generation of prosperity, economic growth had begun to decline. It has been a lackluster 2 percent since the middle of 1984.

These negative statistics came in long after Reagan had been reelected in a landslide. And the aura of his success lasted even longer and was far from dissipated in 1986. Even when the bad news became impossible to avoid in the middle of 1986, there was little sense of what it might mean.

A *New York Times* article by Peter Kilborn, in July 1986, was a typical response to the discovery that all was not well. "Just six months ago," Kilborn wrote, "everything looked so good. Interest rates, oil prices, and the dollar were all down, and many economists, expecting better days, applauded the luck and work of Ronald Reagan. But by summer, the economy had turned resoundingly weak. And the President's economic record had suddenly been thrown into doubt."

But six months earlier—or even at the very height of Reagan's success—there were good reasons to doubt the president's record. There were, for instance, regional depressions and a strangely intractable poverty in the midst of a remarkably uneven recovery during its strongest phase. But economic analysis in recent years has usually ignored underlying structural tendencies and focused on yesterday's indices from the Bureau of Labor Statistics. During the Reagan recession, there were those who thought that all of the unemployed were headed to the poorhouse; and during the Reagan recovery many of those same people believed that all of our fundamental problems had been solved.

In contrast, this book is an attempt to describe the "history" of the future it proposes. That is, it seeks to understand our economics and politics within the framework of complex forces that are radically transforming the very conditions of our lives—and of the world.

I

The West is living through an economic and social crisis so unprecedented in its tempo, so complex in its effects, that there are many who do not even know that it is taking place. They are waiting for an old-fashioned apocalypse, or gleefully proclaiming that there never will be such an apocalypse, even as a gradual revolution mines the ground under their feet.

There has not been, and there probably will not be, one dramatic day such as that "Black Tuesday" in 1929 when the stock market collapsed. The net output of the economy has declined by a percent or two during the recessions of the last decade or so, but it certainly has not been cut in half as it was during the first years of the Great Depression. Even the severe downturn of 1981–82, the worst since the thirties, had a jobless rate less than half that of the earlier catastrophe.

Moreover, in the Depression it was hardly necessary for social critics to write books making subtle arguments about the existence of the crisis. Breakdown was a palpable fact of everyday life and eventually stimulated rank-and-file citizens to take part in great social movements. As a result, the country was finally forced to create a welfare state and pioneer in new modes of government intervention in the economy. Without fully understanding what it was doing, or intending all of the consequences, America not only changed its occupational structure, but its culture, its values, even its sexual mores.

Ever since then, 1929 has been a kind of benchmark, a point of comparison for all political projections. At the worst, there was—and sometimes still is—a vulturelike attitude on the part of some of the opponents of the system: If only things could get bad enough, if only economic collapse would destroy popular illusions, *then* progressive solutions could be easily defined and implemented. In fact, the thirties themselves never followed that simplistic scenario and the eighties are even less likely to do so.

On the Right, many have adopted the quantitative obsessions of the liberalism they hate. They talk endlessly of the jobs generated under the Reagan administration without even noticing that the nature of those occupations is evidence that the crisis is deepening. They rejoice that the thirties—and the seventies—will not return and ignore the looming problems of the eighties and nineties.

And yet, the contemporary crisis is more radical than the Great Depression of the thirties or the "stagflation" of the seventies. When it is resolved, America—and the world—will have been more fundamentally transformed than they were fifty years ago. But this will probably happen within the context of what the French economist Alain Minc has dubbed the "slow 1929." There will be basic shifts in fits and starts, an upheaval in installments, a sea change beneath a surface that is sometimes deceptively calm.

This is not to exclude the possibility of a spectacular economic collapse. For one thing, confident predictions are impossible when, as is now the case, the future is so unlike the past from which it emerges. For another, writing today, it is not difficult to see the possibility of an explosion. To take but a single, quite believable, future: Industrial nations trying to cope with the crisis could adopt "beggar thy neighbor" policies to export their difficulties; the end of the American recovery could set off a collapse of the international financial system and cause bank failures throughout the advanced world; and so on.

But in the "slow 1929," that kind of breakdown is less likely, in good measure because of institutions created to deal with the original 1929. The president of the United States, no matter how conservative he or she may be, is not going to dress for dinner in the White House to inspire confidence, as Herbert Hoover did, if the system starts to crumble. There will be aggressive counter-measures. But, even more important for this analysis, even if the unlikely occurs and the roof falls in on the Western economy, the event will be a belated consequence of the unprecedented crisis, not, as in 1929, a major cause of it. One way or another, we must deal with a problem that is more like cancer than dynamite.

Let me take one example of the nature of the crisis. I begin with the proverbial tip of the iceberg.

The Reagan recovery of 1983–84 was, as I have noted, extraordinarily uneven. There was the strongest rate of economic growth since the Korean War while a depression continued to blight the lives and communities of hundreds of thousands of people in the industrial heartland. There were millions of new jobs, and that fact was the centerpiece of the Reagan reelection campaign of 1984. But at the same time several million workers were pushed down toward poverty and some were forced out of the labor market altogether. Pop sociologists announced nothing less than a new class of young urban professionals even as soup kitchens proliferated.

There are prosaic explanations for all of these facts which have nothing to do with the notion of a crisis of any kind. These contradictions can be seen as the one-time consequence of an overvalued dollar that won a socially cruel war against inflation. The fate of industrial workers can be blamed on their own greed in pricing themselves out of the market and thereby preparing their own painful day of reckoning. It has even been argued that poverty persisted in the recovery because the antipoverty programs had been too generous.

I reject these analyses, but not because they usually come from conservatives (some liberals are, we will see, among the chief proponents of this Panglossian wisdom). Indeed, I will shortly insist on the relevance of some of the conservative accounts of the crisis and even argue that, in everything but basic values and policy conclusions, they bear a striking resemblance to left-wing theories. What is wrong with the accounts of the crisis just cited is that they treat it as an accident, a mistake, or both. They do not understand that what is happening is a basic structural change in Western life.

The fact is, *the nature of economic growth has changed.* Investment can now create more national product but not more jobs, or at least not more jobs of the kind essential to upward mobility for the great mass of the people. That trend took very distinctive forms—one American, the other European—and the Reagan administration wrongly cited the difference to prove the superiority of the conservatism of the New World over the *dirigisme* of the Old.

In the United States there was a tremendous growth in employment, but it was concentrated in the relatively low-paying—and low productivity—service sector. That is one of the reasons why, in Edward Denison's very careful analysis, the rate of growth declined even as one of its major causes, employment, increased during the seventies.* And, as we will see, this development has enormous social and political implications for the future as well. It is a harbinger of continuing crisis, and not, as Reagan and company claim, a sign that the new age is at hand.

In Europe the same problem takes the more straightforward form of unemployment. Margaret Thatcher described it quite well in a 1985 interview with *Business Week*: "Since then [1981] we've been coming up steadily, and productivity is 15.5 percent above the previous peak, and in a way that explains why we've got a greater amount of unemployment." Note well: Increased productivity "explains" growing unemployment. From the point of view of the Great Prosperity after World War II, that is sheer nonsense. Productivity then paid for higher wages, more invest-

---

*I have some fundamental methodological disagreements with Denison, but they are not relevant to the point cited here. He is also a mainstream liberal of the Brookings Institution tendency and, as I will make clear, I have even more basic differences on that count. At the same time his work is outstanding. More broadly, throughout this book I will often quote those with whom I disagree—for instance, sophisticated conservative publications such as the London *Economist*, the *Financial Times*, and *Business Week*—on the grounds that a consensus among my principled opponents on a specific issue is more persuasive than an agreement between my friends.

ment, and enlarged markets in a "virtuous circle" of economic change in which growth caused more growth and employment. Now, however, increasing productivity can eliminate jobs.

Thus the conscious wisdom of the past fifty years, and the unconscious premise since the Industrial Revolution, so well summarized by John F. Kennedy—"A rising tide lifts all boats"— is no longer operative (and never was as universal as Kennedy and economists of the sixties thought). Economic progress can now be the cause of social marginalization rather than of social integration.

Why this is so leads us to the complexities of the rest of the iceberg—and to the rest of this book. But if it is true, then Mr. Reagan's ebullient confidence that his administration has found the path to a new future is badly misplaced. And, at the same time, the economic and political basis of the Western Left for the past half century—the link between economic growth and social justice—is, in its traditional form at least, going, going, gone.

This analysis of the "slow 1929" will lead me to two distinct, and even somewhat opposed, theories about the coming of the next Left.

On the one hand, a recession, even if it is only a "normal" phase in the business cycle and not the immediate result of the structural problems I will describe, could reveal some of the profound fault lines within the system. The recovery, then, would be much more difficult than in 1983, for a modest increase in unemployment in the United States could now lead to a federal deficit of $300 to $400 billion. Under such circumstances, the Right would be discredited and the Left would have the opportunity to present an alternative. But only if it has one.

On the other hand, let us assume for a moment that Reagan has blundered into a genuine new period of expansion which will also work to the advantage of the European economies. It would be, if my analysis is right, as uneven as the recovery of 1983–84. That is, unemployment might "merely" hover around 7 percent (which not too long ago would have spelled a deep recession). The top 20 percent of the society would enjoy a very real prosperity, the middle would live under tolerable but deteriorating conditions, and the bottom third would eke out a precarious, even desperate, life. There would not be the pervasive disillusionment with the Right that might well accompany a straightforward recession. But neither would there necessarily be social peace.

There is a vulgar economic determinism that thinks that bad times lead to radicalism and good times to conservatism. In fact, there is no simple relationship of any kind, but the exact opposite of that proposition is closer to the truth. The militant movements of the Depression, above all the mass industrial unionism of the CIO, did not emerge when things were at their worst, but only when the economy had begun to improve under Franklin D. Roosevelt's direction. They surged forward in 1934 and 1935, not in 1930 and 1931. Terrible times are usually a cause of social retreat and private despair, of alcoholism and child abuse, rather than of brave struggles.

More to the present point, the last time there was a left-wing era in American life, during the sixties, it coincided with the high point of the greatest advance in living standards that history has ever known. And the rebels were not only the black poor of the South under the leadership of Martin Luther King Jr., but also privileged college youth throughout the country. If economic growth is particularly outrageous and unjust, it could well provoke the next Left into existence.

At the end of 1985, the very sober analysts of the London *Economist* were speculating about just such a return of the European Left. "After ten years in eclipse," the *Economist* wrote, "hopes are brightening for democratic socialists in Western Europe. The glimmer of better election chances as conservatives tire is an obvious reason. But a deeper and more intriguing one is a fresh optimism that comes from acknowledging past errors and dropping old certitudes. . . . [N]eosocialist ideas (with a small *s*) are bubbling up which could offer voters a genuine alternative to neoconservatism."

Europe and North America obviously have significant political differences, not the least of which is the absence of a mass socialist movement in the United States. And within North America itself there is a very real sense in which Canada is more politically advanced than the United States. It has, for instance, a labor-based social democratic party, the New Democrats, who get around 20 percent of the vote in federal elections, and, for that very reason, it also has a national health system. During the 1981–82 recession, workers south of the border lost their medical coverage along with their jobs, while those north of the border kept their health protection as a right of citizenship.

But one element in the *Economist*'s comment is at work in America in its own distinctive way. Here, too, there is a cyclical character to the rhythms of Left and Right. As Arthur Schlesinger, Sr., described it, a period of social creativity eventually exhausts itself and its partisans and gives way to a time of consolidation that, in turn, accumulates its own problems and provokes a return to the Left. Let me simply hint at how that thesis might well apply to the not too distant American future.

Ever since V. O. Key first established the model in the fifties, American political scientists have been describing our politics in terms of periodic "realignments" in which new issues and political forces combine to create a framework which then endures over a series of elections. A Republican era began in 1886 and lasted until 1932; a Democratic hegemony started with Roosevelt and persisted through the Kennedy and Johnson administrations. Since the election of 1968, the American Presidency has been the fief of conservatives who have won it four times out of five. This realignment did not, however, extend to the Congress, where the House remained nominally Democratic and the Senate did not fall to the conservatives until 1980. It was, the shrewd rightist Kevin Phillips has said, a "split level" realignment.

Phillips and others believe that this conservative impulse was playing itself out in the mid-eighties. In 1984, for instance, Ronald Reagan was infinitely more popular than either his party or his program. But there was a secret that was kept from the people and probably from the president himself: that his announced program had, as we will see in detail, failed miserably. Mr. Reagan wears the emperor's clothes, and even if he maintains the illusion throughout his second term, his successors will not. When this startling news is revealed, it will give a certain political and cyclical nudge to the structural economic factors.

But then let me add a complication, for we are moving into areas not really charted by any of the old theories. When Reagan, or his legend, come to grief, it will not mark the failure of traditional conservatism but of a kind of rightist radicalism. For the fact is that in 1980 Mr. Reagan was the candidate who said that there had to be fundamental departures and who, in 1981, made some of them. Could it be that Ronald Reagan represented the visionary phase in the movement of that famous political pendulum and that disillusionment with him will make the people intransigently centrist?

I doubt it. The Right shared in Reagan's glory and it will participate in his downfall if, as I am convinced, such a downfall takes place. At that point there will be an opportunity for the Left—but that does not mean that the Left will take it.

II

The next Left could fail for a number of reasons: because its political base is eroded by the very evolution of society; because it does not understand that a radical increase in popular participation in economic and social, as well as political, decisions is a practical necessity; or simply because it isn't sufficiently creative and/or lucky.

The possibility raised earlier—of a society established by an affluent elite and an unhappy but not desperate middle, while the bottom is marginalized—is not simply morally intolerable. It also threatens to destroy the social base of the Left. If it were to come to pass, socialists in Europe and Canada—and liberals in the United States—might still win political victories, but they will have to adapt to a political reality that contradicts their basic principles. That immemorial Western dream that the valleys shall be exalted and the high places made plain, would turn into a mere utopia. And we would not speak of the next Left but of the last Left.

Poor people who are in the mainstream of a society can be a mighty historic and democratic force, as the ragged workers in the dark satanic mills of the Industrial Revolution proved. But functionless people do not constitute social movements. That is why in George Orwell's *1984* the "proles" were exempt from the totalitarian discipline imposed upon the members of the ruling party. They were a miserable anachronism in the electronic nightmare. If the next period were to turn a third or even a quarter of the people in the West into just such an irrelevance— and even if they were pensioned off with welfare payments to keep body and soul together—the Left would no longer have the political possibility of challenging the established order.

The moment would signal the end of the American dream, too. This country is, in social terms, the most left-wing nation on the face of the earth.

We often fail to recognize that fact because the United States is, in political and legislative terms, the most backward of advanced societies. It is the only developed capitalism without a significant socialist movement; its welfare state was not only the last to emerge in the West, but remains the meanest and cheapest, the only one without a national health system. It is, I have already noted, to the right of Canada, which is one reason why union organization increased in that country even as it declined in the United States. And in foreign policy America too often plays the role of Moscow under the Czars: as the friend of global counterrevolution, of Chiang and the South Vietnamese colonels, of Batista and Marcos, and most recently of the contras trying to overthrow the Nicaraguan government.

But at the same time, American society—our manners and our mores, the way we speak to one another and even the refusal of waiters to be obsequious—is as radical as our politics are moderate to conservative. We inscribed upon the Great Seal the words, A New Order of the Ages. Pragmatic and anti-ideological, we are still the only Western nation based upon an ideology. There is no American ethnicity, no "nationality" in the European sense. Even if we honored the principle in the breach as far as blacks and women are concerned, we are united by a democratic ideal rather than by a gene pool and a cultural inheritance. We are the people of the book, of the Constitution.

And we are, in Gertrude Stein's inspired phrase, the oldest people on the planet for we have lived in the future longer than anyone else. Moreover, we have been rich and unique enough to act on leftist values in a rightist way, to create, as Leon Samson so aptly put it, "the socialist version of capitalism." In Europe socialism began as a civil rights, not an economic, movement, dedicated to the revolutionary proposition that even a worker could be a citizen. In Canada the New Democratic Party managed to unite the prairie socialist impulse of radical farmers, a trend that was once fairly powerful in the United States, with the militancy of a labor movement that counterposed itself to middle class liberalism as well as to conservatism.

Here, workers—or rather, white male workers—were citizens almost from the very beginning of the Republic. Our class struggles were more bitter than those of Europe, even though the workers of the Old World acted in the name of an anticapitalist ideology. Our social legislation was inferior to that in the rest of the West and our living standards higher, at least for those who were not abjectly poor. Moreover, even though our social mobility was never as great as most people thought, it was quite real, the basis of what Robert Heilbroner has called the "economic patriotism" of Americans.

So the very social and economic changes that could put an end to the Left would finish the American dream as well. Both developments are, alas, to be taken as serious possibilities.

The Left could also fail because it does not understand its distinctive role in coping with the radical future now underway. It is not simply the proponent of economic planning, of public priorities as opposed to private profit, of a new productivity through tapping the suppressed creativity of the people. It is for these things in a unique way: through the transfer of power to men and women at the base, to "ordinary" citizens. Before those who want to protest that this is a creaking, ancient utopia rise up, let me hasten to agree with them. I would only add that it is also now a *realpolitik*.

I learned a good part of this lesson from conservatives. For in the course of my work I was struck by the remarkable similarity between the analyses of the contemporary crisis by the serious Right and the serious Left. Yet there is a gulf which separates these seemingly convergent points of view, and in understanding its nature—in understanding what the Right is—one grasps the specific role of the Left.

Claus Offe, one of the most brilliant contemporary democratic Marxists in Germany, remarked in a 1980 essay that it is quite possible that the tax policies of the welfare state have acted as a disincentive to investment and that social entitlements have functioned as a disincentive to work. Just because reactionaries insist upon these points for their own cruel purposes, Offe remarked, is no reason to ignore them.

Another contemporary democratic Marxist, Manuel Castels, described how the Keynesian state financed war, welfare, and "unproductive" jobs through debt. He then wrote, "the 'monetary school' is not wrong when it claims that its statistical findings establishing the correlation between inflation and the expansion of the debt and money supply are valid." There is, then, no difference between this Marxist and Milton Friedman? Not at all. Castel continues, "But such a 'discovery' is a blind observation as long as it is not put in the broader context of the dynamics of accumulation in advanced capitalism." Castels is obviously not Friedman—and yet he can recognize Friedman's analysis and even incorporate it into his own.

But then, the Left-Right convergence is not simply analytic and intellectual. It even extends to policy proposals, and here a careful understanding of how similar ideas are fundamentally different helps the Left define its unique identity.

Just prior to World War I, Henry Ford anticipated John Maynard Keynes. Or perhaps he borrowed from Karl Marx, who predated Keynes in some of his insights. Mass production, Ford said, requires mass consumption, which means higher wages. Belatedly—in fact, after the families of workers striking against his company were massacred—John D. Rockefeller agreed. Indeed, this strange history is so important that, as the next chapter will detail, I call the economic, social, and political transformations of the thirties and forties, "Fordism." For now, what is the significance of a Ford embracing the Marxist-Keynesian theory of the need for mass consumption as capitalist productivity develops? It is that Ford wanted this change without any interference from unions or government, as part of a manipulative paternalism; and that the Left struggled to make the same reform through expanding the reality, rather than the illusion, of popular power.

The wily genius of the assembly line agreed with the Left on everything but the essentials.

Recently, in 1985, General Motors and the United Automobile Workers (UAW) concluded a contract for the production of a new automobile, the Saturn. The contract provided for a salary rather than an hourly wage and for job security under almost all circumstances for most of the employees. There would be worker participation in decision making at practically every level; work teams would elect their own leaders; and 20 percent of total income would depend upon productivity and profits. Had General Motors suddenly been converted to anarcho-syndicalist notions of cooperative work?

Hardly. Profound changes in the methods of industrial production had made the old, hierarchical work patterns unprofitable. The company now sought to utilize the individual creativity of the worker for the very same reason that, more than a generation ago, it built assembly lines that stifled that creativity: to make money more efficiently. This is not to suggest that the executives in the front office were moral monsters whose actions can be explained in terms of a single, crass motive. It does argue that, whatever other complexities were involved, including sincere belief in worker participation, that single, crass motive dominated the "bottom line."

The Saturn is scheduled to be made in the most computerized, robotized fashion possible. It will, therefore, reduce the number of work hours per car, which is the key to its profitability. That, in turn, will cut down on the size of the work force in the future, quite possibly giving rise to a well paid, shrinking elite of privileged workers. Had the union, then, simply become the puppet of management? Not at all. It sought to gain as much leverage for its own goals, including the humanization of work, as was possible under difficult bargaining conditions. Its refusal to do so would have almost certainly led to the export of *all* those jobs overseas.

So which side prevailed in the contract? We will know after time and struggle have made a definitive reading of the fine print. For the fact is that in the eighties as in the twenties, what seems to be the same idea can be the vehicle of opposing world views. To simplify, but not too outrageously, the difference between the sophisticated Right and the Left in the next period is between top-down and bottom-up versions of quite similar proposals. It is the same difference, in utterly new form, that divided Henry Ford and the industrial unionists who organized his plants.

Let me generalize. Every serious social idea in the contemporary world leads a double life. This is not because some mysterious symmetry is at work, but because only a very limited number of changes have any significant chance of succeeding. So the Left and the Right necessarily explore a relatively narrow range of possible futures and, when they are serious, respond to the same reality in fundamentally different ways.

Strangely enough, the mainstream liberals—the heirs of the Kennedy-Johnson years—disagree on this count with both the Right and the Left. There is no structural transformation going on in the eighties, they say. If there were a bit more growth and lower exchange rates for the dollar, they argued in 1984, the nation could get back to patterns of happier times. "Recent experience," a group of Brookings scholars wrote, "does not suggest that structural forces are operating to reduce the output of U.S. manufacturing." This is the liberal equivalent of Herbert Hoover's faith that, between 1929 and 1932, prosperity was just around the corner.

I share a more radical sense of what is happening with a conservative such as Frederich Hayek. Hayek argues that the same factors that stimulated the prosperity of the fifties and sixties led to the stagflation and uneven growth of the seventies and eighties. This book offers a proposition that might seem very much like his: that the transformed economic, social, political, and cultural relationships which built the basis for the greatest boom in history eventually undermined that boom. What, then, is the essential difference between us?

For Hayek and others like him, the Left violated eternal laws of economic human nature, and its fall was only a matter of free-market fates punishing Keynesian hubris, as in a Greek tragedy. For the Left, reform had indeed collided with the structural limits of the system it improved, but those limits were, and are, historical, changeable. The conservative analysis points inexorably toward a retreat to the *status quo ante* where a blessed equilibrium, historically as elusive as the Holy Grail, will be miraculously found. For the radical critics of that *status quo*, the only hope is to change structures, to shift the limits of the possible to the left.

The next Left could fail if, like the mainstream liberals, it ignores the structural nature of the crisis, or if it backs off from the advocacy of that bottom-up democratization of the economy that is precisely what separates it from the shrewd Right.

And finally, the Left could use a bit of luck.

I do not say this as flippant truism but as the result of a careful reading of the ideological history of the leftist surge of the thirties. I wish I could report that in those days the Left had thought its way through the crisis and come up with global proposals based on a penetrating assessment of the situation. That could justify the hope that, in our "slow 1929," history could once again be made rationally.

Only it didn't happen that way at all. With one important exception, the West improvised, muddled, and blundered its way into the greatest expansion ever. If, as Michael Piore and Charles Sabel have pointed out, what happened was not exactly an accident—we can observe *ex post facto* a certain structural logic at work—neither was it a matter of design. Indeed, some of the most important innovators, like Franklin Roosevelt, were not at all clear about what they were doing.

I do not think that the future will be made according to a blueprint—whether mine or someone else's—and I do indeed hope that luck helps the next Left as it did its predecessors of the thirties. But an idea or two might nudge the odds a bit. For I am frightened by the prospect that the next Left could indeed come to power—and not know what to do.

III

I write with a sense of urgency since I think the opening to the next Left will take place in a matter of years, not decades. So I want to speak to a broad audience of concerned men and women about a decisive moment in our history that will be affected by how they and others respond to it. I do not believe that this can be best done by a scholarly approach even if what I write is based on the best available scholarship. There will be no footnotes and I will carefully avoid all the details and debates that, in another context, might be of enormous importance.

One might say that this book is a "translation" of an important body of scholarship, most of it—but by no means all—from the serious analysts of the contemporary Left. The reader is therefore warned that I will borrow heavily from others, usually without specific citation. My aim is not to write a work of pathfinding originality but to make some very significant ideas accessible to a larger audience.

It is, then, necessary to analyze the development of a society, not just of an economy. And I will deal with the past in order to face the future. I take the subtitle of this book—*The History of a Future*—with utmost seriousness. That is, the policy concepts that I propose to deal with the crisis are not simply the children of my wish. Rather, they follow from the historic analysis of the rise and breakdown of "Fordism" and of both the conservative and Leftist responses to it.

And finally, those concepts describe *a* future, not *the* future. For several futures are possible now. The one urged here is formulated in what I hope is the authentic spirit of the Left: that the crisis may be turned into an opportunity for human emancipation and social justice, so that the best values of the West can thrive in an unprecedented setting and reach out to help a world in need.

2

Fordism

The crisis of the eighties is the result of the breakdown of the incredibly successful response to the crisis of the late twenties and thirties.

The economic and social events of the last fifty or so years in the West are so complex that a library of analysis will not even begin to exhaust them. There is, however, one theme that is particularly relevant to grasping the contemporary predicament: the rise, triumph, and decline of "Fordism."

The fact that Leftist historians have named an entire era, usually associated with the victory of their own ideology, after one of their arch foes, the capitalist's capitalist, Henry Ford, suggests a phenomenon that bursts the bounds of conventional categories. Why this homage to an inspired genius and ordinary crank, a man who fought unions with a private army and believed in high wages, a technological revolutionary who hated bankers, Jews, Catholics, fat men, and doctors? Even more to the point, Henry Ford campaigned bitterly against Franklin Roosevelt in 1936. Isn't it absurd to call this political period, which Roosevelt so clearly initiated, after Ford? Not at all. Ford, as I have noted, was the first man of power to recognize the basic principle that was to give coherence to the New Deal—a coherence that Roosevelt himself understood most imperfectly. Even before World War I, he had defined and acted upon his radical principle: that mass production demands mass consumption of a new kind. To be sure, he abominated the way in which FDR eventually put his idea into practice. But even so, his idea and his attitudes not only illuminate an age he did not like but helped to create. They also are essential to understanding how we got to where we are in the 1980s.

I

Between 1890 and World War I, Western capitalism made a quantum leap. Henry Ford was one of the first to see how dangerous that accomplishment was.

Before 1890, America was in many ways the most capitalist of societies. There was no residue of feudalism to taint the system in the New World. A myriad of small producers used fairly simple tools constantly adapted to the imperatives of supply and demand. If they guessed wrong, they submitted to the summary justice of the market. As a result, there were, between 1800 and 1900, no less than eighteen panics, depressions, recessions, and stock market collapses. From 1873 to 1897, just short of a quarter of a century, the bad years far outnumbered the good.

But then, starting in the 1890s, there was a profound transition. It was organizational, political, social, economic, and technological. Beginning with the railroads and telegraph, and spreading rapidly throughout the society, there was a new type of economic structure: the corporation took over from the entrepreneur. The individual businessman operating in a restricted area with a modest capital gave way to regional, and even national, organizations managed by hired professionals who spent large sums of other people's money.

At the same time—as both cause and effect of that first transformation—technology began to change. Where small numbers of relatively skilled workers had been able to change their output in response to economic ups and downs, there were now larger and larger concentrations of semi- and unskilled workers using huge machines that could turn out only large batches of standardized products. Not so incidentally, this happened during the high-water mark of European immigration when there were malleable new Americans grateful for jobs in grim factories. Native-born craftsmen thought that their skills had been devalued by the competition of hordes of hungry aliens; in fact, it was the emergent era of mass production that undercut the artisans.

That shift in the scale and nature of production meant, among many other things, that the old way of regulating the system no longer worked. In that free-market period, an unstable equilibrium was occasionally achieved through constant crises of over- and underproduction. It was, Karl Marx remarked wryly, as if the law of gravity proved its validity by the roof falling in on your head. But now there were massive investments in huge plants dedicated to making those standard products. The rigid nature of this technology made the old modes of adapting to supply and demand impossible. And periodic business failure had become too expensive a way to correct imbalances and misallocations.

Now economic crisis threatened centralized, concentrated corporations like United States Steel, and not merely a hundred individual blacksmith shops. The rude discipline of Adam Smith's invisible hand would have been ruinous for such a corporate America with its irrevocable outlays in costly machinery. As Alfred Chandler has documented, one of the distinctive functions of the corporation was to advance the principle of the "visible hand," of the rational control of markets rather than of blind obedience to them.

Henry Ford responded to this challenge more profoundly than anyone else.

Not that Ford invented the new technology. He borrowed the concepts of sheet-metal stamping and electric welding from the producers of bicycles and sewing machines; he took the idea of continuous-process manufacture from cigarette makers and distillers, refiners, and meat packers. But he synthesized the innovations of others as no one else had ever done, mechanizing the very flow of production as well as its individual components. The

Model T factory was the most productive the world had ever known, and the Model T's themselves were the first really cheap durable goods for consumers. So Ford's assembly line, refracted through the tragicomic brilliance of Charlie Chaplin, came to stand for the quintessence of an age.

Were that all he did, Ford would have gone down in history as an inspired engineering genius, but not as the man who antici-pated principles of economic and social organization that were to dominate half a century of the nation's life. That latter claim arises because Ford understood that his technical breakthroughs required a transformation of the society, not just of the factory or even just of the economy.

"In underpaying men," Ford said, "we are preparing a gener-ation of underfed children who will be physically and morally un-dernourished; we will have a generation of workers weak in body and spirit who, for this reason, will be inefficient when they come into industry. It is industry which will pay the bill." But Ford did more than simply talk about the necessity of decent wages. He paid five dollars a day in his own plants and was attacked by some of his fellow capitalists as a "socialist" for doing so.

The idea that the workers had to be paid enough to "buy back" what they had produced was hardly new. It had been a staple of leftist agitation among the workers for almost a hun-dred years before Ford, and was the most popular simplification of Marx's complex analysis of capitalist crisis. There had even been a few employers in the nineteenth century who said that the system needed a well-paid labor force with sober consumption habits. Indeed, there was a bit of schizophrenia in every busi-nessman on this count: As a producer, he wanted low wages to minimize costs; as a seller, he wanted high wages to create a larger market and maximize sales.

Henry Ford went well beyond all of his precursors. First, he actually paid the high wages. Secondly, he saw the link between wages and productivity in a manufacturing process that sub-jected workers to severe physical and psychological demands. Management's decency to workers would increase output; a little justice would yield a lot of profit. Thirdly, Ford created his own distribution system of franchised automobile dealers, and began to provide cheap credit to the masses so that they could buy his cars.

There was also a puritan aspect of this philanthropy. Ford created a "social" department which visited workers' homes and checked out their habits: whether they were properly married, were religious, maintained neat houses, drank, gambled, and so on. There was a premium wage which was only given to those who met strict standards. In short, Ford saw his wage policy as part of a drive for a new, controlled style of working-class life, of higher consumption, but of the "right" kind. Aldous Huxley was quite right to invoke his name as a patron of the behaviorist dictatorship in *Brave New World*.

Ironically, it was a Marxist genius in Italy who was one of the first to grasp what the capitalist genius in America was doing. Antonio Gramsci was the leader of the Italian Communists and was jailed by Mussolini. While in prison, he wrote a series of notebooks—they take up four printed volumes—in which he commented on events outside the walls. In 1929–30, he reflected on "Americanism and Fordism." Perhaps, he speculated, Fordism might constitute a new "historic epoch," a "passive revolution" in which basic economic and social change occur, but without a political explosion like the one in France in 1789.

Fordism, Gramsci wrote, was associated with a new "programmed" capitalism. It was American in that it occurred within a society without feudal traces, which could therefore "rationalize" production as the Old World, with all of its historic encumbrances, never could. In part, it was the result of shrewd economic policies: Ford's transportation and distribution network, Gramsci said, gave him the extra profits that allowed him to pay high wages. But the analysis was most profound in insisting that Fordism was cultural and psychological as well as economic.

"In America," Gramsci argued, "rationalization has created the necessity of elaborating a new type of man, conforming to a new type of labor and production process." It was not an accident, he thought, that Ford was so interested in the drinking and sexual habits of his employees—or, for that matter, that the triumph of Fordism in the twenties coincided with Prohibition, making access to liquor difficult. "Animality" was the enemy of the scientifically organized work process. Therefore, the high wage and the new consumption patterns were an "objective necessity for modern industry."

It was true that, in the United States of the 1920s, the 15 percent increase in the real income of working people allowed them to buy the new consumers' durable goods of the age—the radio, the phonograph, and, above all, the car. Moreover, that change meant that the workers were now more likely to spend their free time in the private enjoyment of their new possessions—or in going to the movies—than at the union hall, the saloon, or a political meeting. The Depression brought repossession of some of those goods by the finance companies, and politicized the lives of those who lost them. But after World War II, that passive and manipulated consumerism feared by Gramsci and sought by Ford came back with a vengeance.

Ford's fellow industrialists were not as insightful as he, but they, too, flirted with what David Brody calls "welfare capitalism." In 1913, John D. Rockefeller expressed shock when company thugs and militia set a strikers' tent colony afire and suffocated two women and eleven children at his family's mine in Ludlow, Colorado. In part, his response was pure public relations in the face of a public outcry. He proposed to the nation the "Colorado Industrial Plan"—or the "Rockefeller Plan"—to give representation to the workers in the management structure. Communication between employers and employees, he said, was the key to industrial peace. During World War I, the War Labor Board took up that thesis and required more than a hundred corporations under its jurisdiction to recognize workers' committees.

After the war, the idea of "industrial democracy" swept through the upper reaches of big business. At Jersey Standard, the Rockefellers not only gave their workers a voice but provided accident benefits and paid vacations as well. The financier J. P. Morgan said that the major corporations had to learn to cooperate with one another and their workers. In 1922, the new president of General Electric announced that "relations with the men" were as important as the costs of production.

This was the era in which Harvard psychologist Elton Mayo scientifically established that treating employees like human beings would increase productivity. And an exceedingly liberal Republican, a one-time supporter of Teddy Roosevelt and a U.S. presidential candidate favored by the *New Republic*, assembled industrialists of "advanced views" and told them that they should "establish liaison" with the American Federation of Labor. His name was Herbert Hoover, and Franklin Roosevelt said of him in 1919, "he is certainly a wonder and I wish we could make him president of the United States. There could not be a better one."

In 1921, now secretary of commerce, Hoover convened a conference on unemployment that explored the possibility of using public works as a part of a countercyclical strategy against joblessness. He also worked out industry "codes" to eliminate unfair competition, an idea that would be central to the National Recovery Administration (NRA) of FDR's first New Deal. Above all, Hoover agreed with Ford: Capitalism had to have high wages if it was going to survive.

Fortune magazine summarized this corporate wisdom in 1931: "To the new capitalism, the wage earner is a purchaser, a partner and the key to production. . . . His wages are dictated . . . by ambition for a market and a desire for willing cooperation. . . . The new capitalism . . . is a social conception as radical as Stalinism in its ultimate purpose."

Europe, Left and Right, agreed. André Philip, a French socialist scholar, came to the United States in the twenties to study the labor movement. His description of Fordism (which Gramsci used as the basis for many of his speculations) sounds like a 1980s American book describing productivity breakthroughs in Japan. On the right in France there were "neocapitalists" who tried to learn from the American experience. They believed that "the Americans have demonstrated the obsolescence of a capitalism that postulated scarcity." Prosperity, they said, would eliminate "the evil shepherds who live off the misery of the workers."

Most impressive of all was the fact that, when the Crash did come in 1929, big business tried to live up to its new creed. President Hoover urged the corporations to maintain high wages and many of them responded positively. The layoffs in the first year and a half of the Depression were not, for the most part, in basic industry. U.S. Steel, for instance, kept 94 percent of its employees on the payroll through January 1931, by rotating the work even though it was only operating at 50 percent of capacity. Ford himself answered Hoover's plea in 1929 by paying seven dollars a day.

Hoover, true to his planner's notions about capitalism, created the Reconstruction Finance Corporation (RFC) to invest government money in private banks and thereby stimulate the economy. Later, the RFC was taken over by Roosevelt, and, in a considerably changed form, made a central component of the New Deal. In the 1980s, there are serious business people—most notably, the investment banker Felix Rohatyn—who see the revival of the RFC as an answer to the current crisis. In this case, then, the left-right convergence is as obvious as a Hoover innovation that became a part of the New Deal program.

So Henry Ford's Fordism was an extremely powerful idea— but ultimately it could not work in the form that he proposed.

His version of the idea required the voluntary cooperation of business as a whole, but only some of the most prosperous captains of industry were persuaded by it. It is, to put it mildly, difficult to achieve a consensus within a class in which everyone is competing with everyone else. Secondly, as the economist Sumner Slichter wrote at the time, these programs were designed to prevent workers "from becoming class-conscious and from organizing unions." They were taken seriously mainly when there was discontent to be defused, and as soon as that was accomplished, old-fashioned authoritarianism took off its democratic mask.

It was, in short, impossible for a conspiracy of private employers to change the wage structure of the United States so as to create vast new markets and at the same time maintain paternalistic power over the workers. When the stock market bubble burst, the basic reality of American society was precisely the one feared by Henry Ford: a productive system whose output far outstripped its consumption capacities. On the surface there were many continuities between the early New Deal and the corporate panaceas of the twenties. But there was one huge difference.

Franklin Roosevelt proceeded to "nationalize" Henry Ford's idea and to do so in alliance with a militant labor movement that Ford fought at every turn. The social contract was rewritten, but without the participation of business, David Rockefeller was to say, looking back from the sixties. And yet, if Fordism was thus ushered in over the violent objections of Henry Ford and his friends, Gramsci turned out to be quite right. The resultant upheaval, for all of its struggle and violence, created a system that served upper-class purposes even as it recognized working-class rights. It was not a conspiracy of the rich, since most of them had angrily excluded themselves from the process, but even so, it worked to their advantage. Even if he didn't know it, Henry Ford left his imprint on the system.

II

If I have implied that the New Deal took over Ford's ideas, I have oversimplified. Neither Franklin Roosevelt nor most of the European Socialist parties consciously created a Fordist society. If they did indeed carry out a momentous change in the conditions of Western life within the framework of a profoundly modified capitalism, they were not entirely clear about what they were doing. This may be a depressing fact in the context of this book, but it is necessary to learn from it.

When the Depression hit, the Socialists of Europe were already in the middle of an unnerving experience: They had won power in a number of countries after World War I, but did not have a very good idea of what they were supposed to do with it.

In the three-quarters of a century between the Communist Manifesto of 1848 and World War I, those Socialists were outsiders, agitators, critics. They mobilized the anger of the masses against a system for which they had no responsibility and in the process made telling critiques of it. When the workers finally got the vote and actually won some seats in European parliaments, there was the very perplexing question of how they should exercise their new, and very partial, power. But they were in a minority and thus could paper over the fact that their classic doctrines—Marxism very much included—were silent about what to do in that *terra incognita* located between capitalism and socialism.

After the war, things got worse: Government power was thrust upon the Socialists in Germany, Austria, and Britain, and they were briefly part of the ruling majority in France. They didn't know how to make a "revolution," which in any case was not on the agenda in the West. Moreover, the Soviet experience began to make them wonder if they wanted a revolution, and it was clear that the majority of people did not. What, then, were socialists to do with capitalism?

In practice, many Socialist governments resolved these problems by being leftist in social policy, increasing various benefits for the workers, and scrupulously orthodox, even conservative, in their economic strategy. They insisted, in the name of Marxism, that capitalism had to be run as capitalism, which meant balancing the budget and all the rest. When socialism came sometime in the dim and blurry future, there would be production for use instead of for profit. For now, bourgeois prudence was the order of the day. So it was that, in Britain in the twenties, the Labour government was attacked from the Left by the Tory maverick Harold Macmillan. It was also deserted by one of its own leaders, Oswald Mosley, who, disgusted with the Labour Party's paranoia about deficits, eventually became his country's leading fascist.

The major attempt to theorize a way out of this embarrassment was made by Rudolf Hilferding, one of the most serious Marxists since Marx. He rightly explained that *laissez-faire* was over, that an "organized"—statist and imperial—capitalism had taken its place. He wrongly concluded, however, that capitalist planning had so ameliorated the economic contradictions of the system that all the socialists had to do was to take it over democratically. Then, in 1929, "organized" capitalism began to fall apart. The socialists faced a catastrophic confirmation of their worst fears, but without knowing how to act on their hopes.

Since they proposed a vast increase in unemployment benefits *and* a balanced budget, all that was necessary was to square a circle.

Hilferding marvelously formulated the bankruptcy of his own synthesis of "evolutionary Marxism and free-enterprise economics." In an angry exchange with trade unionists who wanted an immediate response to the crisis in 1932, that venerable Marxist said, "Depressions result from the anarchy of the capitalist system. Either they come to an end or they must lead to the collapse of the system." Keynes, a partisan of the British Liberal Party, responded to a similar comment from the leaders of the Labour Party with the exasperated comment that his concern with unemployment made him "the only socialist" in the discussion.

The Swedish Socialists were an exception to the rule. The "School of Stockholm" gathered together an extraordinary group of Left economists, such as Ernst Wigforss and Gunnar Myrdal, and they made their own very socialist, even Marxist, interpretation of Keynes. They were the only political movement in the thirties that carried through a deficit-financed socialization of consumption as a means of stimulating production in a conscious and planned fashion. The policy worked.

That, too, simplifies. The European trade unionists, as Mario Telo has shown, were moving in a Keynesian direction, even if in a confused way, and in Germany W. S. Woytinsky proposed public works and cheap money as a way out of the impasse. And in Britain, a number of younger Socialist leaders—Hugh Gaitskell, Evan Durbin, Douglas Jay, and Hugh Dalton among them—introduced the Labour Party to the Keynesian ideas that would prevail after World War II.

In France, Léon Blum, who followed Roosevelt much more carefully than did his Swedish comrades, attempted a Keynesian recovery. He remarked that he was following the same path as FDR, but, while the American president improvised, he was acting on the basis of a plan. However, and the fact emphasizes the accidental character of the emergence of the Keynesian age in the West, Blum's theory-based policies didn't work while Roosevelt's improvisations did, at least to a certain degree.

Roosevelt, for that matter, never really got over his orthodox and very pre-Keynesian convictions. In his first months in office he had, under the influence of the doctrinaire Lewis Douglas, deflated! He was very late in coming to support the Wagner Act, an institutional commitment to a collective-bargaining process that was essential to the postwar boom. And his obsession with balancing the budget set off a steep recession within the Depression in 1936–37. Keynes met Roosevelt once, in 1934, and afterward commented to Frances Perkins, the secretary of labor, "I don't think your President Roosevelt knows anything about economics." And finally, it was, of course, the "War Deal," not the New Deal, that put an end to the Depression.

When the war ended, everyone, even the Swedish Socialists, prepared for the return of the thirties. That did not happen, and the West discovered, to its surprise, that it had somehow stumbled into the greatest economic expansion in history.

I stress the rather inglorious character of this history, whether American liberal or European socialist, for quite contemporary reasons. First, it mandates a certain humility. We don't know exactly why ideas that didn't work in France in 1938 were a success in 1945. Secondly, if a "leap" from capitalism to socialism, or even from an outlived capitalism to a more liberal version of the system, is simply not possible, that means that reformers will always find themselves on hostile terrain. They must introduce new principles into a powerful and established structure. In the process, they will face the dangers of failure and success: of failure, because the old order simply will not tolerate sudden increments in social justice and will malfunction in its own defense; success, because when the leftist changes do work, the Right, once it gets over sulking, will co-opt them.

III

At no point in the thirties did any major politician in the United States or Europe proclaim, "We shall abolish the ancient dictum of St. Paul that he who does not work shall not eat!" Or, to put the matter more prosaically, there was no serious proposal to transform the nature of the wage system under capitalism. That, however, is what happened.

After World War II, a person's wage in the West was no longer the sum of money that he or she received in a pay envelope. It now included a whole series of financial claims upon the government and it continued to generate income long after a person had stopped working altogether. In the case of Survivor's Insurance, a worker continued to provide for his or her heirs even after death. The wage had become the social wages and that meant that a significant portion of national income had been removed from the cycle of boom and bust.

In the United States, the social wage took the form of direct transfer payments, like social security and Aid for Families of Dependent Children (AFDC); of military spending; of outlays for health and education; of tax subsidies; of the government's impact on the old-fashioned wage bargain itself. Each of these measures raised, or maintained, the buying power of the citizen-consumer in the Keynesian society. It was widely thought that the poor got the best of this deal when, as we will see, they actually got the worst. In fact, the social wage tended to have the same maldistribution as private income and wealth.

The wisdom of each program can be debated, but the macro-economic effect is beyond dispute: This was the fulfillment of Henry Ford's dream of stable markets, but it took a partial socialization of consumption to achieve it. It was the reason why, when the war ended, there was the Great Prosperity instead of the return of the Great Depression.

In examining the development of the social wage, I will not focus primarily on the statistics, even though ignorance of them is a major source of reactionary illusions among the American people. Rather, I am concerned to show how Henry Ford's values survived and prospered in genuinely progressive programs created as a result of social struggles from below. The point is not one more muckraking tour of the welfare state, but to prepare the way for a structural analysis of the contradictions at the root of the present crisis.

The Social Security Act of 1935 was, and is, the centerpiece of the American welfare state. It, and allied programs for the aging, account for about two-thirds of domestic social expenditures.

In its first phase, social security was counter-Keynesian. That is, American workers and employers began to pay into the system in 1937, but the benefits were negligible until the early fifties. The first effect of the law then was to depress consumer demand, to tax rather than to spend, but it eventually became a central measure for the direct socialization of consumption.

Even when social security did begin to pay out substantial amounts of money, it was still partial in its coverage: Only about two-thirds of paid employment was under the program in 1950, and some of the excluded, such as farm workers, were among the poorest in America. And the money received by the retirees was quite modest: an average of $74 a month in 1960 ($241 in 1982 dollars) as compared to $419 in 1982. That escalation was basically accomplished in the early seventies by indexing somewhat more generous benefits to protect them against inflation. President Richard Nixon opposed the reform, then took credit for it in a communication to the recipients right before the election of 1972.

The consequences of this change were, and are, startling. Monthly social security benefits were about 20 percent less than the median weekly wage in the fifties and 20 percent more than that median in the mid-seventies. As Robert Kuttner summarized the trend, "Thus, over a twenty-year period, social security pensioners increased their incomes by about 40 percent relative to wage earnings—during a period when real wages were rising rapidly as well. . . . In 1960, the average social security check for a retired couple equaled 50 percent of the official poverty level. By 1985, it exceeded 85 percent."

There is an important political complexity in this recent history and it is death to any simple determinist account of social policy. In the United States and Europe, the big increase in social outlays did not take place in the sixties, the social decade par excellence, the time of upheaval and protest. It occurred in the early seventies, when the illusions of endless growth were still alive but the conservative reaction was beginning to set in. Between 1960 and 1981, our social spending went from 10.9 percent to 20.8 percent of GNP, *mainly in the form of those increased social security benefits.* In France the comparable rise was from 13.4 percent of GNP to 29.5 percent, in Holland, from 16.2 percent to 36.1 percent. And Canada, so similar to the United States in so many respects, was as usual somewhat more generous than this country as its outlays climbed from 12.1 percent of GNP to 21.5 percent.

Why did the United States suddenly become so generous (although, as these figures show, it remained relatively stingy compared to the Europeans and Canadians)? In part, the phenomenon was cause and effect of a momentous social change: a shift in family life, with the government taking on the responsibility for the care of the aging. That, in turn, had a double economic effect. The aging received their checks—and their children, free from at least part of the burden of taking care of their parents, could now spend more money on themselves. A widespread misunderstanding also played a role in the popularity of the program. Most Americans wrongly thought social security was an insurance system in which one got back what one paid in, with interest.

In fact, social security in the United States is not "funded" at all. That is, the government does not put aside current contributions and invest them to meet future obligations; it spends them on the present generation of retirees, and those workers who are contributing to the system now will have to depend on the willingness of the next generation to pay for them when it is their turn to retire. Moreover, there is a distinct "welfare" element in the system for two groups, the poor and the rich. But, and this is a crucial factor, the bulk of the benefits, even though they are not allocated fairly, go to the middle class. That is why there is no stigma in taking them.

The pre–social security income of the American aging leaves about 30 percent of them poor; but after the benefits are paid, their poverty is reduced to 15 percent. That is, at least 70 percent of social security expenditures goes to people who would not be officially poor even if they didn't receive them. Moreover, the system is financed through a regressive tax which makes it a bargain for the upper middle class and the rich. But if one leaves equity aside, social security eventually made a massive contribution to creating a sector in American society in which income is not based on work, or even upon the contributions of the participants when they were working, but depends upon the decisions of Congress.

And yet if social security, probably the fairest of the welfare-state programs, still pays considerable homage to Henry Ford's business priorities, the history of health care takes that tendency to an extreme that borders on caricature.

During the New Deal, there were serious proposals from within the Roosevelt coalition to make national health a part of the social security bill. But the resistance of the American Medical Association (AMA) and the conservative wing of the Democratic party effectively scuttled the idea, which was never even sent to Congress. Fifteen years later Harry Truman tried to revive the program, but the false charge of "socialized medicine" defeated it in a Cold War era during which anything "socialized" was supposed to be a Soviet import.

It took thirty years after passage of the Social Security Act to achieve a partial national health plan: Medicare for people over sixty-five, and Medicaid for some of the poor. Even that was achieved because organized medicine had become much more "Fordist" in theory and practice over the intervening years.

Private insurers, like Blue Cross and Blue Shield, now loomed large. They were not about to fight socialized insurance premiums. Hospitals had become more important than the doctor's office and they, too, took an institutional view of the subsidies they could get. The result was the worst of capitalism and the worst of socialism combined: Third parties paid for fee-for-service medicine and no one was particularly concerned about controlling the outlays or quality. So the United States, with less public health care than any other Western nation, spent more of its GNP on medicine than any other—11 percent.

The ultimate irony was that the AMA and the medical profession now participated enthusiastically in a process that justified the worst of their ancient fears. It had always been said that a national health program would destroy that famous institution, the family doctor. Now that Washington was pouring tens of billions of dollars into Medicare, impetus was given to the "industrialization" of medicine. Corporate hospitals and suppliers turned into giant entities, and in 1984–85, merger conversations between several of them involved the creation of a health business with more than $5 billion in "sales." *Forbes* magazine reported that the Republic Health Corporation was "figuring out the costs and profitability of performing, say, tonsillectomies and coronary bypasses."

Social security and Medicare were then the almost universally popular core of a welfare state that became increasingly unpopular. The reason for this paradox is to be sought in "entitlements."

The "entitlement" programs, above all those means-tested measures that support the poor, are routinely thought to constitute the bulk of the welfare state and to be the cause of its fiscal overload. That is simply not true. In 1984, the age-tested expenditures, which go mainly to the nonpoor, cost $289.2 billion. The "welfare" programs—AFDC, food stamps, child nutrition, housing aid—received $39.4 billion. So "welfare" accounted for about 12 percent of the total, and the real value of its benefits has been declining since the late sixties. There was a distinctly Fordist aspect even in this sector. Food stamps, perhaps the most effective social program of the past quarter of a century, is also a guaranteed market for corporate agriculture (that is why the recipients are given stamps, good only for food, rather than cash).

"Direct benefit payments to individuals," then, take the lion's share of welfare state expenditures. In the 1986 budget from an exceedingly conservative administration, they amounted to 41 percent of the total—compared to 29 percent for defense. That constituted a massive socialization of consumption and it was primarily spent on the aging, i.e., on the nonpoor. Even here, where Fordism straightforwardly increased the social wages (as opposed to the market wages), market priorities played a major role. But despite this patent—and publicly ignored—unfairness, these programs were a major advance over the pre-Roosevelt inequities.

More to the point, these outlays were a major reason why the

Depression did not return after World War II. For the next half a century, the West was no longer haunted by the specter of under-consumption. The conservatives of the eighties, we will see, may, however, have begun to reverse that historic trend.

IV

The Right railed against the social programs and almost always got the numbers wrong. The one form of socialization it endorsed enthusiastically was, of course, military spending. But then the Left's attitudes in this area were sometimes confused. It often rightly fought against escalations of the arms race that threat-ened the national security of the United States and the very exis-tence of civilization. But then it simplistically concluded that those unconscionable policies must also be the prime cause of our economic troubles. That was, and is, not true, and it is important to put that fact into perspective.

The basic argument against military spending must be politi-cal. That is, had it been necessary to introduce a draconian—but egalitarian—regime to defeat the Nazis, I would have supported massive cuts in social spending. And even if I thought that the cold-war expenditures had promoted growth, full employment, and worked against racial and gender discrimination, *but at the price of risking World War III*, I would have opposed them. And similarly, just because the arms race should be fought, in the name of sanity, at every turn, does not mean that all of its eco-nomic effects are necessarily bad.

War and the welfare states were linked together well before the Soviet-American conflict. World War I showed that, despite the claims of free-enterprise ideologues, government could orga-nize the economy effectively. In the United States, for instance, the tradition of top-down, technocratic planning goes back to the mobilization of the economy in 1917–18. On a more benign level, the First World War also convinced militarists and governments that, on grounds of national security, they could not tolerate bad health on the part of a population that had to supply a conscript army. Indeed, there was a short and incredible period right after

the armistice when the AMA was in favor of socialized medicine
for that reason.

World War II put an end to the Great Depression in the
United States because it justified a government intervention so
much more massive than anything Roosevelt had proposed in
peace time. As a result, there was genuine full employment—a
jobless rate of around 1 percent in 1944—and women and minorities made the greatest percentage gain in income ever.

During the Korean War, military spending as a percentage of
the Gross National Product (GNP) rose to a cold-war high of
about 13 percent and undoubtedly acted as a powerful Keynesian
stimulus, generating jobs and income. But from that time to the
present, that percentage has never approached that level. Even
during the Vietnam War it was under 10 percent and by the mid-
seventies it had dropped to less than 5 percent. Therefore it is
inaccurate to say that military spending—or a nation in thrall to
the "military industrial complex"—is the prime cause of either
the postwar prosperity or the crisis of the seventies.

That is not to suggest that arms outlays are socially neutral.
They are unquestionably that form of social spending that, as the
means of destruction became more and more sophisticated in
their deadliness, does the least to generate jobs. During the past
two decades, the military has been buying excessively ingenious
high technology, which requires the talents of engineers and very
skilled workers who already have jobs, not the hard-core unemployed in the ghetto. And there is no doubt that the *immediate*
cause of the inflation that signaled the beginning of the end of the
postwar euphoria is to be found in an unpopular and immoral war
that Lyndon Johnson could not finance by a tax increase. Moreover, the fact that so much of the money and talent for research
and development has been lavished on overkill rather than, as in
Japan, on peacetime uses has made America less competitive in
the world market.

Military spending, then, was an often economically and socially perverse, but secondary, element in promoting and abort-
ing the postwar expansion. Viewed in its own right, it was the
most insane public investment of the age, but that does not make
it the main cause of all our woes.

V

There were two other ways in which the government shaped the income structure to suit its purposes. They are, for quite different reasons, not often recognized for what they were and are.

The socialization of the income of the rich has received much less attention than social security or AFDC. It is indirect, hard to see; and too much candor would be embarrassing to the recipients. This phenomenon was not even quantified until the 1960s, when the idea of a "tax expenditure" made it possible to define an entire area of government largesse.

The familiar Keynesian fiscal policy stimulated the economy through spending and broad tax cuts that increased global demand. Tax expenditures, in contrast, reduced the amount of taxes that *certain* classes of citizens had to pay the government in order to promote *particular* kinds of production and consumption. In 1988, for instance, it is estimated that three deductions to homeowners will save them $60 billion that they would have otherwise had to pay to Washington. The rationale is that society wants to encourage both home ownership and construction.

The problem is, homeowners and investors tend to be much better off than the population as a whole. Moreover, the bigger the house or the investment, the larger the tax subsidy. That is, these expenditures increase along with wealth and do nothing for the poor and very little for working people and the middle class. Not so incidentally, their total cost far exceeds that of all the poverty programs in the budget.

Ronald Reagan's "supply-side" nostrum took these exceptions to the rule and turned them into the rule itself. But then, in 1985 and 1986, the same Ronald Reagan who had radically redistributed income upward, from the poor, the workers, and the middle class to the rich, suddenly turned into a tax "reformer." It is a tribute to the credulity—perhaps the gullibility—of the American people that they believed him. But since the Democratic party did not comment on Reagan's masquerade, that was not too surprising.

The 1986 tax law is a new, seemingly fairer variation on the old injustice. First, a significant number of poor people are being dropped from the tax roles altogether, which is obviously quite positive. Few noted that this was primarily a rectification of the outrage that saw the taxes of the poor radically *increased* in the early eighties. In 1979, federal income taxes started, for a four-person family, at $1,214 *above* the poverty line; in 1982, the levies began at $1,135 *below* that line! So Mr. Reagan and the Congress were widely applauded for undoing an injustice that they themselves had committed.

Second, Mr. Reagan has indeed proposed to deprive business of certain tax deductions, like the investment tax credit. In the main, this move will hit classic Fordist enterprises in the declining manufacturing sector, which invest heavily in plant and equipment, and will improve the relative position of high-tech firms that never benefited from the earlier provision. Some of the most shocking tax shelters were also eliminated, since, from a sophisticated corporate point of view, they clearly squandered funds on totally nonproductive uses. These moves, in short, updated but did not change the fundamental principle that the government should subsidize capital.

Third, the rich were compensated for all of their lost deductions by radically lowered income tax rates. That is, at the very most there had been a certain redistribution of tax privileges within the upper class but no shift at all, as between the upper class and the rest of the society. Outside of a few radical critics of this sham reform, only Richard Musgrave, one of the most respected of mainstream experts in this area, pointed out that the emperor—or rather, the president and his bipartisan accomplices—wore no clothes. The "reform," Musgrave documented in the *Wall Street Journal*, did not really change tax burdens at all. The income of the rich, I would put it, remained "socialized" in much more generous fashion than that of anyone else in the society—in classic Fordist fashion.

Fordism also transformed the old-fashioned wage contract between worker and employer.

The Wagner Act was passed in 1935, making it public policy to settle labor disputes through collective bargaining; in 1938 a minimum wage was established and the regular workweek was limited to forty hours. These statutes did not immediately or necessarily have an impact on the wage relation. American employers engaged in a war of uncivil disobedience against the right of union organization even after it was enshrined in the law; the minimum wage has varied over the years in real terms, that is, it declined as a percentage of the average wage during the seventies, from 50 percent to 42 percent; and in recent years the enforcement of the wage and hour regulations has been so lax it permitted the return of sweatshops.

The complexities were not, however, all negative. Between 1940 and the late sixties, collective bargaining was one of the most important means of socializing the wages of American workers.

There was a decisive moment in the process during World War II, but practically no one recognized its importance at the time. There were controls of both wages and prices to fight inflation. However, in the war-induced, full-employment economy, unions were in a powerful position. One way to offset the conflict between union strength and wage controls, the War Labor Board decided, was to allow a 5 percent rise in the "deferred wages" of fringe benefits. After all, future payments for postwar pensions, health care, vacations, and the like would not bid up wartime prices.

That fateful decision was made all the more important shortly afterwards when the Internal Revenue Service—one of the most significant policy institutions in the United States—ruled that employer contributions to those fringes were not to be taxed as part of the workers' current income. That meant that the best organized workers could, for instance, find a collective bargaining solution to the absence of a national health system and that the impetus to fight for such a system was reduced.

By the seventies, about 6 percent of the income of Americans derived from fringe benefits. As long as there was no prolonged unemployment, this portion of the society's buying power was put on a long-term basis, independent of the ups and downs of the business cycle. Indeed, unemployment compensation was celebrated by everyone in the fifties and sixties as a "built-in stabilizer" of the economic system.

At the same time, there was a tendency to relate workers'

pay to productivity. In 1948, the UAW and General Motors made a trend-setting agreement: Wage increases would be determined by the rise of productivity in the economy as a whole. That idea had been around for some time, and the Council of Economic Advisors, newly created under the Employment Act of 1946, had been pushing for it. It was based on the assumption that, if only labor and management would act reasonably, there could be permanent, noninflationary growth.

If, it was reasoned, the workers demanded wages higher than productivity gains, that would create income in excess of the goods upon which it could be spent and would lead to inflation. But if the workers were paid less than their productivity, that would lead to production in excess of the society's ability to consume and thus to recession. If, however, both sides agreed to a measured, steady pace of wage increases, then management would have more profits and labor more money. The issue of social justice—of how much the adversaries "should" have in a proper distribution of income—was declared irrelevant. For even if the slices of the economic pie were unfairly allocated, so long as it kept growing, everybody's slice would be bigger every year.

The UAW contract, as Michael Piore and Charles Sabel have shown, became a kind of benchmark. The other big unions struggled to get as much as, or more than, the UAW. In the unorganized sector, those managements that carefully increased wages in line with union settlements in order to keep the organizers out were also affected. And, in theory at least, the minimum wage put a floor under the exploitation of the most vulnerable workers.

During the Kennedy-Johnson years, the notion of productivity-based wages became official policy. There were annual "guidelines" indicating how much management should pay and labor should demand. And there was "jawboning" as Washington, with considerable power at its disposal, tried to persuade the two sides to follow its recommendations. In a famous incident, steel executives who double-crossed President Kennedy in this area felt the full fury of the White House, compelling them to roll back a price increase.

During the Great Prosperity, then, both business and labor

assumed that there would be annual wage increases and, since the optimistic ideology of the times assumed that growth would continue forever, no wage cuts. Relative wages between industries had fluctuated wildly before 1948 and hardly at all afterwards. There was, as Piore and Sabel put it, a de facto "Keynesian incomes policy."

So it was that throughout the West, the "nonwage" labor costs in manufacture—the employer's contributions to various social insurance funds and, in the United States, to fringe benefits—grew enormously. Between 1965 and 1978, they were 26 percent of total wages in this country, 51.4 percent in Italy, 43.7 percent in France and 40.8 percent in West Germany.

Thus, as Goran Therborn, a Swedish Marxist, has pointed out, by the end of the seventies in the West, income deriving from the government (either through direct public employment or transfer payments) was substantially higher than the total of dividends, interest, rent, and entrepreneurial income. Precisely, the conservatives of the seventies and eighties would say. It was the pampering of consumption at the expense of production that eventually led to the crisis.

That analysis has probably persuaded a majority of the American people that the sixties were the triumph of the heart over the head. In fact, during those years it was widely assumed—by business as well as by unions, by the rich as well as the poor—that these programs were the key to prosperity. More to the point, the people who thought that were quite right. Consider, for instance, just one set of figures in chart on page 42.

The period of Fordist triumph was, then, the time of the greatest capitalist success in a century. It was, as the statistics on world trade show, a time of phenomenal expansion in that sector. But that does not mean, as some critics of the Western impact in the Third World think, that it was the exploitation of the poor of the globe that was the decisive stimulus for this great advance.

There is no doubt that the have-nots of the planet made a significant—and outrageous—contribution to the haves in this period. Throughout the boom (with two brief exceptions, during the Korean War and in the early seventies) the terms of trade

AVERAGE ANNUAL GROWTH RATES IN
WORLD INDUSTRY AND TRADE

PERIOD	WORLD INDUSTRY	WORLD TRADE
1860–70	2.9%	5.5%
1870–1900	3.7	3.2
1900–13	4.2	3.7
1913–29	2.7	0.7
1929–38	2.0	−1.15
1938–48	4.1	0.0
1948–71	5.6	7.3

were very much in favor of the advanced nations, i.e., the prices they received for their manufactured goods rose relative to the prices they paid the Third World for its raw materials and agricultural products. There was, then, a very real transfer of wealth from societies still confronting the problem of starvation to affluent countries in which dieting was becoming a national obsession. And the new international economic institutions—the World Bank, the International Monetary Fund, the General Agreement on Trade and Tariffs—were all designed and run by the West, with little interference from the world's poor.

But there was an even more significant shift which was much more important as a stimulus for the boom: The rich countries now invested more in one another than in the poor lands. The Fordist societies were growing at such a rapid pace that there was more money to be made by their investing in each other's affluence than in speculating on the poverty of the Third World. "West-West" trade increased much more rapidly than exchanges between North and South. Lenin's theory—that mature capitalism could not find outlets for its own profits within its boundaries and would be forced to enter upon a ruinous national competition for such opportunities in Asia, Africa, and Latin America—no longer applied.

At the same time, and once again in flagrant contradiction of the conservative myth of the seventies and eighties, Presidents

Kennedy and Johnson unleashed a "supply-side" boom in the sixties. Kennedy introduced depreciation allowances and investment tax credits that President Eisenhower had refused to advocate on the grounds that they were too blatantly pro-business. And there were other subsidies for capital in the Kennedy-Johnson tax cuts.

In the first five years of the sixties, net nonresidential fixed investment (the best index of "capital") averaged $20.5 billion a year in 1972 dollars; in the second half of the decade, when the Kennedy-Johnson policies came on line, the figure was $42.5 billion a year. And throughout the entire postwar prosperity, one of America's most important industries, agriculture, was mechanizing at a faster rate than industry, not the least because federal support programs provided the richest farmers and the agribusinesses with subsidies to do the job.

So the postwar years saw intensive, mass-production techniques spread throughout the entire Western economy. In the United States, capital investment per worker went up by 2.7 percent between 1950 and 1975, in West Germany by 5.2 percent and in Japan by 9 percent. Given the resulting productivity gains, it was possible to increase direct and indirect wages—the money wage and the social wage—regularly while the real price of labor went down. That was, so to speak, the squaring of the circle: Labor costs went up by 2.29 percent, but output rose by 4.16 percent. Business could make money by paying its employees more!

So the mass production and consumption dreamed by Henry Ford took place on a scale he never could have imagined. Workers could afford washing machines, refrigerators, cars, and, with federal tax subsidies, even a house in the suburbs. This change, however, was not simply economic. It was profoundly social as well.

VI

It is a cliché that this period, and particularly the sixties, saw a spiritual and psychological change as well as an unprecedented material advance. I suspect that many do not realize how profound, and even surprising, that stale truism is: Business people, mainstream economists, and government administrators participated in the *Zeitgeist* along with student radicals, hippie freaks, and dropouts. The "straights" in that unlikely coalition have carefully repressed the memory of their sixties fling. It was, however, an essential part of the Fordist ethos.

Most of the social changes were, and are, obvious enough. The number of college students doubled between 1960 and 1970. That was not, as is often said, the consequences of the "baby boom" but of the baby boom *and* an economy that could afford to exempt a growing number of young people from the necessity of working. It was furthered by massive governmental subsidies, justified—more often than not—on the grounds that such "human capital investments" would pay off in the growing productivity and higher tax revenues that educated workers would create.

The momentous transformation of the position of women in the society also began during those years. One reason was the relentless commercialization of all of life; another was that the new consumption standards of the Keynesian society demanded at least two incomes per family in an America that was much less affluent than most people realized. The number of married women in the paid labor force in the sixties went up by one-third even as the female college graduate discovered that she was subjected to systematic discrimination. Nevertheless, one of the most immemorial of authoritarian relations, the subordination of women to men, began to shift.

Indeed, all of the social movements of the period were focused on noneconomic demands: racial and gender equality, ecology, an end to *in loco parentis* on campus, opposition to the war in Vietnam. All of this is familiar enough. What is not understood is that the Left, Right, and Center participated in the same euphoria.

Max Ways was the resident thinker at *Fortune* magazine during the sixties and therefore one of the most significant corporate ideologists in America. He, as well as many other people in business, was persuaded by the thesis—developed by Daniel Bell in academia—that the "end of ideology" had occurred. Since the society had discovered a way to promote constant growth through the cooperation of once antagonistic social classes, economic and social life were no longer a "zero-sum game" in which the losers paid the winners. Now, everyone could win so long as they obeyed the new rules.

At the same time, Daniel Patrick Moynihan, then a high-level bureaucrat in the Johnson administration, argued that one of the problems of the future would be how Washington could learn to spend money fast enough. For if the GNP kept growing and growing, federal revenues, even with tax cuts, would rise, too, and if they were not rapidly plowed back into the economy, that would have a deflationary effect. Paul Samuelson, the most influential economics teacher of his generation, as well as a nobel laureate, wrote of the future in the 1967 edition of his basic textbook: "The United States . . . can hardly help but grow at the rate of 3.5 percent or more, even if we do not rouse ourselves but merely keep our system working well. If we do rouse ourselves and do things which can speed up growth, a 4 percent-plus rate ought to be well within our grasp."

The flower children, student revolutionaries, and ghetto militants believed Samuelson. Dropouts assumed that endless productivity would allow them to retire to a comfortable, but rebel, margin of the society. Herbert Marcuse, the guru of the student radicals, asserted that automation held out the promise of rapid liberation from menial and demeaning labor, indeed for the "reign of freedom" prophesized by Marx at his most utopian. And some blacks thought the society so rich that it was realistic to demand reparations for the centuries of racism.

All of this led to the most unlikely united front in recent American history: the Johnson campaign of 1964. Supporting the Democratic president against a free-enterprise ideologue were Henry Ford III, Walter Reuther, the leading liberal trade unionist of the time, and Dr. Martin Luther King Jr., as well as the main white student radical organization, Students for a Democratic Society (to be sure, SDS qualified its backing; instead of the standard "All the Way with LBJ," it was for "Part of the Way with LBJ"—but that included voting for Johnson).

Corporate America began to pretend in the seventies that the social spending of the sixties had been imposed upon the nation by irresponsible leftists. In fact, those policies, in mid-decade at least, had the support of almost everyone in the society, big business very much included, and the only dissidents were isolated rightist ideologues.

For old Henry Ford had grasped something profound and the Great Prosperity had acted on his wisdom, even if against his will and without knowing too clearly what it was doing. He deserves to have an age named after him, because he, rather than Keynes or Marx, predicted what happened: not simply high wages and a modicum of decency for the workers, but those things *in order to expand the power of corporate America*. That is the vision the United States and Europe really acted upon—and it facilitated very real gains even though it was capitalist rather than liberal or socialist.

The growth of the social wage was obviously not *the* cause of all this—there is no single cause of complex historical transitions—but it was the precondition of everything else. Those productivity advances and the economic results of science and education could not have taken place in a society with the social and income structure of 1929. But then, they were not a panacea either. For now we have to turn to the question of why Mr. Ford's marvelous solution broke down in the 1970s.

3

Did the Government Kill
the Goose That Laid
the Golden Eggs?

Fordism worked economic miracles between 1945 and 1970–1975.
Then productivity, profits, higher real wages, and all the other
components of the virtuous circle that created the Great Prosperity went into decline. Stagflation—simultaneous high unemployment and inflation, a theoretical impossibility in the received
wisdom of the sixties—became all too real. The welfare state,
which had been hailed even by business people as a savior,
turned into an economic villain.

Why?

Analysts of the Left, Right, and Center replied that there
had been a structural breakdown, that something fundamental
had gone wrong. Only the mainstream Keynesian liberals, as
noted in chapter 1, denied that proposition. The problems of the
seventies and eighties, they said, were caused by factors external to the system, like the Organization of Petroleum Exporting
Countries (OPEC) price hikes of 1974 and 1979; by one-time
events, like the influx of the baby-boomers—and of women in
particular—into the labor market of the seventies; or by unfavor-
able rates of international exchange that were simply the conse-

quence of a bad monetary policy. So Robert Lawrence of the Brookings Institution wrote in the spring of 1984, when the Reagan recovery was at its height, that the rise in manufacturing employment had been "stronger than might have been expected." In fact, it is now clear that there was *no* increase in the jobs in that sector, or rather that, since the days of the Carter administration, it has lost at least one million places. Lawrence's error was not simply a bad judgment; it was firmly based upon the theory that, as another Brookings essay put it, there is "no evidence" that "structural change is accelerating."

Almost everything that follows contradicts that view, so I will not criticize it in detail at this point. Suffice it to remark that those who had so brilliantly used John Maynard Keynes to amend Adam Smith in both theory and practice were understandably reluctant to admit that their synthesis was coming unstuck.

With this moderate Keynesian exception, the Left and the Right agreed on a basic dynamic: Since the collapse of the expansion came right after its high point, the reasons for its failures were to be sought in the nature of its success.

However, as soon as one tries to get specific about why and how, there are a number of problems that stem from the fact that all the economic determinants of that success had been interlinked, that there had indeed been a virtuous *circle*. Did someone assert that wages had increased too rapidly and thereby disrupted the perpetual growth machine? If productivity had risen even faster there would have been no difficulty at all. But then, wasn't the productivity crisis itself due to a shortage of profits and a resulting fall in investment per worker? And on and on until the analysis returns to where it began.

Even more basically, all of the theories that explained the economic failure of the seventies on the basis of the economic success of the sixties assumed that the latter had pushed the system beyond its limits. What limits? Had the government spent "too much"? In the 1920s, Keynes had told the French that taxes could take no more than 25 percent of the national income without wrecking the system. In the sixties and early seventies, France went far beyond that level—under the rule of the Center-Right—and prospered. William Simon, a conservative Republican, wrote in the seventies that Washington's outlays had exceeded the permissible and then had the candor to admit that he could not exactly say what the permissible was.

That prudence turned out to be well advised. Under Ronald Reagan, whom Simon supported enthusiastically, the federal deficit rose to more than $200 billion in a single year and the national debt grew more under one president than under all of his predecessors. But then such embarrassments are not new. In the seventies, the United States spent less of a percentage of its GNP on social programs than any other major Western power, and Britain was second from the bottom. That did not keep business in both countries from complaining that it was at the mercy of international competitors because of excessive welfare payments at home—even though the competitors were paying for much more expensive social systems.

There is an explanation for all of this indeterminacy. There are indeed structural limits to social change, but they are political, psychological, national, and historical, as well as economic. Contrary to the conservative vision of eternal laws that govern a perennial *homo economicus*, those limits are specific products of a given, changeable system and, in the modern era, of stages within the dynamic evolution of a system. The New Deal was impossible until it worked (indeed, there were those ideological diehards who continued to prove that it was impossible a generation after its success).

In his famous pamphlet, *Imperialism*, Lenin said that capitalism could not possibly raise the living standard of the masses and remain capitalism. The anti–New Deal conservatives, who would have been shocked to learn that their attitudes were impeccably Bolshevik, made essentially the same argument in their tirades against the social programs. The more complex truth was, and is, that there are indeed limits, but that they can be changed by a radical transformation that will still operate within the system.

That happened in the thirties in a basically positive way, as we have just seen. In the seventies and eighties, we have experienced the unraveling of that Fordist solution, but the new version of the system—and its limits—has not yet emerged.

I

The most popular single theory about the crisis is that government intervention killed the goose that laid the golden eggs of the Great Prosperity. True, proponents of this theory say, the New Deal did work for a while, but then the first few drinks make an alcoholic pleasant even as they prepare the way for a lost weekend.

There are three main variations on this theme. Government borrowing for social programs eventually "crowds" the private sector out of financial markets and thus allocates an increasing percentage of the national wealth to nonproductive uses. Second, the high tax rates for those who work, and the easy entitlements for those who do not, act as work disincentives and ultimately cause individuals and the entire economy to lose motivation and drive. Third, Keynesian deficit finance inflates the currency faster than the economy produces goods and services, and rampant inflation is its built-in consequence.

There is no question that social spending increased rapidly in the West, particularly in the 1970s. But when one looks a little closer, one discovers that, between 1960 and 1975, fully half of the 10 percent increase in the Gross Domestic Product (GDP) devoted to such purposes in the major economies occurred in just two years, 1974 and 1975. That was, of course, the time of a deep economic recession. Tax revenues went down because so many people were out of work and unemployment compensation went up for the same reason. In the United States, for instance, the latter payments rose by more than $25 billion between the end of 1973 and the end of 1975. And since government had to finance these expenditures in a contracting economy, its share of the national product automatically went up.

In a mere two years, then, the crisis caused a governmental outlay equal, as a percentage of the GDP, to the stimulus that had led to prosperity during the previous thirteen years. Does that allow one to say that the government was the cause of the breakdown—or were its deficits an effect of it instead? Like the half-full, half-empty glass of water, these questions give rise to reasonable answers that differ profoundly.

Second, the conservative critique of government spending focuses on only one kind of expenditure: help for the poor. And even that element is widely exaggerated because the critics usually forget that about 85 percent of domestic social outlays go to the nonpoor. But there is another, even more important, error. What about government spending for the rich?

I am not simply talking about the tax expenditures for the wealthy described in the last chapter. More broadly, the governments of the Keynesian welfare states systematically socialized the costs and most of the social consequences of private economic growth. That was, and is, one more tribute to the influence of old Henry Ford in the articulation of the New Deal. And it means that a major portion of the social expenditures of the sixties and seventies were imposed upon governments by corporations rather than the other way around. The "fiscal crisis of the state" was, as James O'Connor showed, an inherent consequence of economic growth under such circumstances.

For instance, it was Washington that had to bail out the rail system when private management bankrupted Penn-Central— and then when Conrail turned out to be profitable, the government rushed to turn over a money-maker to the private sector. The Federal Reserve became the lender of last resort that shamefacedly nationalized the Continental Illinois Bank and also saved the many banks that would have been ruined had Mexico defaulted on its debts.

Agriculture is an even better example, for it demonstrates how the costs of growth were imposed upon the public. The quantum leap in the productivity of the American fields was paid for, in considerable measure, by federal subsidies to agribusinesses and large farms. That process displaced hundreds of thousands of small farmers and agricultural laborers, many of whom then became "social problems" when they migrated into unfamiliar cities with little or no preparation for what they would find there. The corporations and the rich farmers reaped a socialized profit; the society had to pay for privately induced problems.

The numbers, it turns out, are a bit more complicated than they might seem at first glance. But there remain the three very specific attacks on state intervention as the cause of the crisis of the seventies. What about them?

II

Was it true that the welfare state, by borrowing to finance the deficits engendered by its own prodigality, crowded the productive investors out of financial markets and thereby weakened the entire economy?

That was a central theme of American conservatives, such as William Simon, starting in 1973 (the ideological onslaught had to wait until the 1972 elections, since Richard Nixon was following an exuberantly Keynesian strategy to return himself to office). Even more important, that thesis became one of the central arguments in favor of "supply side" economics. The liberals, it was said, had subsidized mere consumption to the detriment of investment (the latter is the "supply side") and it was now necessary to reverse those perverse priorities.

The data simply do not confirm the "crowding out" theory. Between 1975 and 1980, corporations were able to borrow $100 billion for stock tender offers that were part of the "paper entrepreneurship" of those times (shuffling the titles of ownership without creating new wealth-producing assets). The idea that there were, in those most uncertain and crisis-racked days, hordes of business people blocked from building new plants and machines because the money had been absorbed by the welfare state is, on the very face of it, preposterous.

The international evidence is even more dramatic proof of this point. During the mid-seventies, when the Chase Manhattan Bank was publishing newspaper ads on how a capital shortage was about to unhinge the economy, it and the other major banks of the West were transferring tens of billions of dollars to the Third World and laying the basis for the global debt crisis of the eighties. In 1970, government and private loans to the developing countries were of roughly equal importance: $33.5 billion in official funds, $34.9 billion from private sources. But between 1970 and 1983, the private bankers pumped twice as much money into the global South as the governments did: $352.4 billion as compared to $175 billion.

All of this was widely celebrated as a triumph of the banking system. The billions of dollars that flowed to the OPEC nations as a result of the quadrupling of oil prices in 1974 were, it was said, "recycled" to the nonoil, poor countries to help them pay their new energy debts and for new investment. This "virtuous" act was, of course, enormously profitable to the banking intermediaries. In 1972, 34 percent of Chase's earnings came from its international operations, in 1976, 78 percent. There was plenty of cash, then, not simply for Mexico, Argentina, and Brazil, but for Zaire as well.

The fact was that at the precise moment when the American banks were supposed to be short of capital because of government borrowing to pay for the welfare state, they were so awash with liquidity that they were scrambling around the world in a desperate search for borrowers.

III

What about the second theory? Did high taxes for the rich, and easy entitlements for the poor, encourage both to shirk work? Did Fordism sap the will of American society?

There is certainly evidence that the tax system and its subsidies for the rich undermined the entrepreneurial drive of American business by providing handsome rewards for tax avoidance rather than productive investment. As noted in the last chapter, when Ronald Reagan proposed tax simplification in 1985, one of his major aims was to stop money from being primarily used to avoid taxes. Needless to say, the president did not dwell on the fact that his own 1981 tax act—the very centerpiece of his first administration—had caused the price of capital to vary from industry to industry on the basis of their particular tax subsidies, and in some cases had turned economically unprofitable investments into government-supported moneymakers.

This is only a single example of the way in which the de facto industrial policy of the United States is usually determined behind closed doors by lobbyists and congressional tax writers. In 1981, however, the supply-side giveaway to the rich was so huge that the Democrats tried to outbid the Republicans in proposing outrageous subsidies. And if Reagan's 1981 law was designed to aid capital-intensive industry, his 1985 proposal to abandon accelerated depreciation had the opposite effect. The very announcement of that move acted as a major incentive to corporate takeover maneuvers in 1985. The corporate raiders wanted to act before Washington took the subsidy away from them.

This problem is not simply American. The concept of the tax expenditure, developed in the United States in the sixties, was exported to West Germany, Austria, Canada, France, Spain, Japan, and Australia. In Canada, tax expenditures and direct government outlays are voted in a single package and there are trade-offs between open and indirect subsidies. Throughout the advanced industrial world, the state is engaged in a difficult struggle to gain control of its own largesse to the corporation.

There is no question that the welfare state for the rich has promoted waste and inefficiency. And since tax expenditures increased much more rapidly than the federal budget in the seventies, this form of government intervention, with wide support in practice from corporate conservatives who oppose it on principle, did indeed contribute to the malfunctioning of the economy during that decade. What about a much more widely discussed and popular subject, government assistance to the poor?

Losing Ground, a book by Charles Murray, had a considerable impact on the United States in 1984. Murray argued that *the* cause of the persistence of poverty in the early seventies, and of its increase after 1979, was that the social programs and attitudes of the sixties had encouraged workers to leave the labor market. His basic methodology was profoundly flawed in that he attempted to present a unicausal explanation of more than ten years of social history. He claimed—wrongly—that the persistence of poverty coincided exactly with the generous Kennedy-Johnson antipoverty programs in the late sixties. Among many other things, he ignored that at that time there were also an acceleration of technological revolution, an unprecedented internationalization of the American economy, a structural rise in "normal" unemployment, and much more. Welfare policy, he said, explained everything, and these massive economic and social trends, nothing.

Still, didn't welfare for the poor persuade them not to enter the labor market? There is no evidence that public policy had a major impact upon withdrawals from the labor force in the United States, but there are some disturbing reports from Europe that point in that direction. The reason for the difference between the Old World and the New has to do with that widely unappreciated, and even unknown, fact: The welfare state in this country is the most minimal in the Western world.

As a result of studies carried out over a decade at the University of Michigan, we now know that the typical mother receiving AFDC benefits—that is the most important "welfare" program in the United States—does not correspond to the popular stereotype of a lazy woman breeding a big family to avoid work. Nor does that woman resemble Murray's somewhat more sophisticated image: an instinctive economist who shrewdly calculates that she can make more money from AFDC, food stamps, Medicaid, and the like than by going out and getting a job.

The Michigan researchers discovered through a "longitudinal" study—they followed a huge, scientifically selected sample over many years, rather than taking polls of different people at different times—that half of the AFDC recipients turn to the program because of a sudden crisis: The father of their child (or children) dies or deserts them; there is a sudden illness; and so forth. These women leave AFDC in less than two years by getting a job, a sign that the Protestant ethic is still with us. Indeed, only 15 percent of the AFDC mothers remain on the rolls for eight years or more and thus conform to the image of the chronic welfare dependent. So Murray explains a fact—how welfare motivates large numbers of people to absent themselves from work—that is not a fact at all.

Moreover, the real value of welfare payments in the United States declined from 1969 to 1984, that is, during the period in which the nation's destructive generosity was supposed to be motivating rational people to choose welfare over work. In the early eighties, the combined real value of food stamps and AFDC was less than the value of AFDC alone in 1969. Ironically, it was the Reagan White House that emphasized this fact in 1985 when it bragged about the administration's accomplishments in reducing poverty in 1984. That year, the Reaganites said, was the first to see a rise in real public assistance benefits in fourteen years. An analyst at the *Wall Street Journal* commented, "so much for Charles Murray!"

This is not to adopt a countersimplification and to argue that federal entitlements never lead people to drop out of the labor market for a period of time. Of course they do. It is simply to assert that in the United States, with its pinchpenny welfare state, this phenomenon is not a significant factor in the economic crisis. In Europe, things are more complex. There, for instance, unemployment compensation often lasts three or four times as long as it does in the United States and provides a much higher percentage of the average wage. In the United States, during the recession of 1981–82, less than half of the jobless received any unemployment benefits from the government at all.

In Holland, the unemployment program in the mid-seventies provided for 85 percent of the average wage (net of taxes) for the first 130 days, and 82 percent after that for up to two years. In that country, more than a quarter of the population between fifteen and sixty-five years of age received some form of transfer payment in 1976 and 1977. Sick leave went up as a percentage of total work hours, from 7.2 percent in 1968, to 10 percent in 1978. There are similar data from Denmark where analyses show that, between 1966 and 1976, a quarter of the employed workers between twenty and twenty-nine years of age got sick pay. As one went up the age scale, people were sicker for longer periods of time—but less often.

The fact that younger people got sick more often than their elders—or, more precisely, got reimbursed for being sick more often—strongly suggests malingering. A sympathetic observer, John Logue, generalized: "The solidaristic values of the generation that built the welfare state (in Scandinavia) seem to be giving way to more egotistical values in the younger generation. There seems to be a long-term rise in the use of social welfare benefits that is independent of objective needs." With universal benefits and high minimums in Scandinavia, Logue argues, the generation that was born into a welfare state created by the struggle of their parents lost some sense of responsibility toward it. It had become an established fact, not an important innovation.

I would put that phenomenon into an even larger context. The welfare state is a hybrid, too socialist to be completely capitalist, decidedly too capitalist to be socialist. In Europe, its founders were socialists who dreamed not simply of an increment of reform, but of a new society with new motivations. In fact, the "social democratic compromise" has only permitted social measures within an extremely hedonistic, individualistic, late-capitalist culture, and the latter always threatens to corrupt the former. It is, I would suggest, for this historic reason that the generational differences described by Logue came into existence. And since there is no prospect of a quick and easy way to go beyond the welfare state, the following irony emerges: The more decent society is *within such a halfway house*, the more likely it is that there will be negative economic effects.

Unfortunately, the United States does not have to worry about this problem too much since it has kept its passion for social decency firmly under control. Therefore, the "work disincentives" of welfare were less prevalent here than anywhere in the West, and do not even begin to prove that a government-induced laziness is a cause of our crisis.

IV

What about the third variation on the government intervention theme: that Fordism is inherently inflationary?

Of course the welfare state is inflationary. There is general agreement on this point across the political spectrum. A Hayek, writing from the monetarist Right, says that "every one of the chief features of the welfare state . . . tends to encourage inflation." Paul Samuelson, speaking for the postwar Keynesian mainstream, concedes that "every mixed economy must face the problem of a tendency for full employment to result in creeping inflation." The big capitalist powers, asserts the Marxist Ernest Mandel, have all "opted in favor of an institutionalized and permanent inflation as a means of dealing with, and preventing, catastrophic economic crises like those of the years 1919–1932."

This consensus obviously conceals enormous differences, not the least because we must ask more complex questions to get serious answers. For instance, what are the alternatives to the built-in inflation of the welfare state? Is that inflation a consequence of social spending, military outlays, and/or policies of cheap money for the private sector?

To begin with, Keynes was well aware that his policies would lead to rising prices—but for him, that was an infinitely lesser evil compared to mass unemployment (which, it should be remembered, had actually begun in the twenties in Britain).

The level of joblessness, the orthodox economists of Keynes's generation held, was determined by the wages demanded by the workers. If millions were in the streets, that was because they had priced themselves out of the market. So mass unemployment was an unfortunate, but necessary, mechanism for bringing supply and demand on the labor market back into equilibrium. That was wrong, Keynes replied. There were workers ready to hire out at almost any price—and no one would take them. The decisive determinants of economic activity were consumption and, above all, investment, which would not be forthcoming unless profits were likely. If government stimulated demand, that would motivate capital to invest and put labor to work. But if there were not sufficient aggregate demand to encourage private sector growth, then the jobless might have to wait forever, no matter how low they set their sights.

Keynes knew that putting money into the economy through deficit spending would have a double effect: an increase in production and an increase in inflation. Indeed, he candidly insisted that the real value of money would fall because prices would rise. Even so, employment would rise, too, and there would be more real wealth as wasted resources, human and material, were put to work.

"Thus," Keynes wrote, "public works even of a doubtful utility may pay for themselves over and over again at a time of severe unemployment . . . but they may become a more doubtful proposition as a state of full employment is approached." That last qualification would obviously take on considerable significance in the late sixties. But in the Depression, the cruel expenditure of unused capacity and jobless men and women was so great that Keynes sarcastically noted that if the government were to fill bottles with banknotes and bury them in idle mines, capitalist enterprises could make money, and the society could gain in wealth by making a business of retrieving them. "It would indeed be more sensible to build houses and the like," he added.

Morally, politically, and economically, Keynes was right, and the orthodox economists, with their Buddhist tolerance for the necessary suffering that must be endured to achieve equilibrium, were wrong. His strategy, we well know, worked and was not even as inflationary as he had feared. Between 1950 and 1969, inflation in the United States was less than 3 percent a year in all but two years. It was higher, but quite tolerable, in Europe because joblessness was much lower in the socialist-led or influenced welfare states than in this country. This was the era of the squared circle when real wages rose but productivity increased even more and profits and workers' income no longer seemed to be antagonistic.

Small wonder that those euphoric theories about the end of the class struggle and the economy as a positive-sum game flourished. Capital had its profits, labor got regular increases in real wages, social spending went up, and there was much talk of how, now that the old-fashioned capitalist problems had been solved, the society could concentrate on the quality of its life. But, as Keynes anticipated, success brought its dangers.

In 1960, the unemployment rate was 5.5 percent, and in 1961, the first year of the Kennedy administration, 6.7 percent. A good part of industrial capacity was idle, so the Kennedy-Johnson stimulus took place under those conditions of wasted human and material resources in which Keynes said even dubious public projects made sense. To be sure, the tax cuts of those years were very strong on the supply side. But still, the income of the people rose steadily and the markets for business were correspondingly enlarged.

Then in 1966, one year after the escalation of the Vietnam War, wages went up by 6 percent, but productivity lagged well behind and unit labor costs increased by 3 percent. The era of the squared circle was at an end, winners and losers began to reappear, and for a very brief time labor got the upper hand in a class struggle with corporate America that had not, as had been so widely advertised, disappeared. Gradually the discussion of inflation began to take precedence over the issue of unemployment.

Was government spending the cause of the inflationary trend that asserted itself in the late sixties? Curiously, there is a united front of some of the Right and some of the Left on this count. They agree that Washington was to blame, but one cites social spending and the other, Vietnam. The Left's simplification is superior to the Right's in that it is partially correct.

To begin with, the overall impact of government spending was simply not that vigorous during those years. There was a "high employment surplus" through 1965 and deficits well under 1 percent in 1966 and 1968. * In 1967—when the economic escalation of Vietnam was most marked—there was a much higher deficit, but it was less than in any year between 1970 and 1975. So it is wrong to say that the problems of the sixties were preceded by reckless government spending.

Social spending did go up between 1965 and 1970, but at a much slower rate than in 1970–75 when it was propelled by the expansion of social security and Medicare. There is no doubt, as I showed in the last chapter, that the unconscionable war in Vietnam triggered the price rise, but it cannot be made the cause of the double-digit inflation that was to take place some years later.

---

*The "actual" deficit is the difference between the government's expenditures and revenues. Both parts of that sum are mandated by the economy, e.g., in a recession, unemployment benefit costs rise abruptly even though Congress doesn't pass a new law. To define the portion of the deficit that is the result of Washington's policies rather than of the business cycle, one computes the actual deficit as a percentage of what the GNP would have been at a high employment level, that is, at a point where those economic factors are without influence on spending and one can measure the impact of government actions alone.

There is even more surprising evidence from Europe. When the inflationary crisis did come in the seventies, a number of the highest-taxing, biggest-spending welfare states on the Continent had price increases at a significantly lower rate than the United States. In a fascinating analysis, the economist Leon Lindberg suggests that this happened *because* countries like West Germany and Austria were quite generous in their social programs. With the workers assured of their basic economic security, they could be much more "reasonable" about wage restraint than their counterparts in the United States, the weakest of the advanced welfare states.

On this count, the monetarist conservatives, who emphasize the money supply rather than the federal budget in their account of inflation, are more sophisticated than the welfare-state bashers of the Right and the antimilitarist simplifiers of the Left. For the private sector was much more profligate than the public in the sixties, and when the crisis came it took all the help it could get from Washington for its own deficit financing. Corporate America's books were more unbalanced than the government's but, needless to say, that did not keep business from lecturing Washington on the need for Puritan economics.

V

In the popular imagination, Keynes was the economist who said that the government should borrow money to subsidize consumption in order to get the economy moving. One cannot blame the people for this simplification since it is a fairly faithful reproduction of the version of Keynesianism propagated by the "official" Keynesians in the United States, the Kennedy-Johnson advisors included. A brief foray into this complex intellectual history is necessary if we are to account for one of the most important sources of our troubles: that even as the establishment was moaning over the government's fiscal irresponsibility it was engaged in creating a "casino society."

After World War II, when a whole host of factors—and not just the theory and practice of Keynesianism—made for an economic boom, the "official" Keynesians, particularly in the United States, made the most conservative possible interpretation of the master's analysis. They even reconciled it with the classic doctrine that he demolished. If, Paul Samuelson wrote on the final page of his famous textbook, fiscal and monetary policy would guarantee high employment, then "that classical theory comes back into its own. . . ." Correct the one glaring flaw in the classic perspective—the automatic tendency toward full employment— and the old, and reassuring, equilibrium model was restored. This is often referred to as the "neoclassical synthesis" and it is the work of Adam Smith's John Maynard Keynes.

So it was that serious scholars actually came to believe in the mid-sixties that they had helped to create the utopia of the classic dream, a permanently growing economy that needed only a judicious governmental shove now and then to achieve its miraculous, but not quite self-regulating, equilibrium. To quote from the last report of the Johnson Council of Economic Advisors, in January 1969: "The forces making for economic fluctuations have been contained through the active use of fiscal and monetary policies to sustain expansion."

For Joan Robinson, the British economist who was one of Keynes's most brilliant associates, such an interpretation of her mentor was a "bastardized Keynesianism." Keynes, she and other Left Keynesians said, never adopted the equilibrium model, even in a revised form. He always understood that a capitalist economy was inherently dynamic and unstable, that the conditions of full-employment success would create problems that would subvert the happy state. Moreover, in the last chapter of his magnum opus, Keynes had explored "the Social Philosophy towards which the General Theory might lead." To be sure, he called his theory "moderately conservative in its implications," but that was in contrast to a completely statist—Stalinist— model of socialism. Most of his social philosophic implications were fairly radical.

Among them were the need for a "somewhat comprehensive socialization of investment," viewed as the alternative to the socialization of industry itself; the creation of an abundance of cheap capital through "communal saving" supervised by the government; and a consequent drastic fall in the interest rate to near zero that would lead to the "euthanasia" of the "functionless investor" and put an end to the thesis that inequality is an economic necessity if there is to be a pool of funds for investment. A member of the Bloomsbury circle, Keynes also thought that once the economic had thus been disposed of, people could get on with the serious things of life, like art and love.

Two American scholars, Theda Skocpol and Margaret Weir, suggest that this left-wing Keynes even had a brief period of influence in the White House. Franklin Roosevelt, we have seen, was a pre-Keynesian traditionalist with very little grasp of the economic theory he is credited with introducing into this country. In the opening years of his presidency, he was much more concerned with the joint regulation of the economy by government and corporations in the National Recovery Administration than with deficit-financed public spending. And even when he turned to the Social Security and Wagner acts in 1935–36—the "Second New Deal"—he still believed in a balanced budget.

But then, in the summer of 1937, there was a new recession within a depression that had never ended. The stock market collapsed again; industrial production, which had almost reached 1929 levels, declined by a third; unemployment soared back up to eleven million workers. Finally, in April 1938, FDR abandoned his antideficit faith and ordered massive (for those times) government outlays. It was at this point that a group of economists around Alvin Hansen at Harvard had some impact with a radical Keynesianism that focused on the structural problems of the system, income redistribution, and still more public spending. But, Skocpol and Weir argue, the institutional power of conservatism, centered in the Congress, prevailed. In any case, military Keynesianism took over within a year or so as Roosevelt turned the nation into the "arsenal of democracy."

The postwar Keynesians in the United States scrupulously forgot the radical side of Keynes and enthusiastically embraced state subsidies for private investment rather than "communal saving." More to the present point, they also ignored one of Keynes's lifetime concerns, the monetary system. There was a reason for this omission, Hyman Minsky notes. Between 1933 and 1966, i.e., throughout the adult life of the sixties Keynesians, there were practically no bank failures, credit crunches, liquidity crises, and the like. That was an accomplishment of the New, and War, Deals. But then, beginning in 1966 and continuing to the present, financial markets have been in almost constant turmoil. The forgotten Keynes provides a suggestion of why this happened—and another key to both inflation in the seventies and the crisis of Fordism itself.

With high levels of employment in a boom, labor's bargaining power improves and this dries up a significant source of profits. The standard business response, to substitute machines for workers, is limited by a number of factors: the pace of technological change, the cost, and a short-time horizon. But the very prosperity that brings these problems is an incitement for further expansion as corporations fight for shares of the growing market. At that point, debt looks like the sword that cuts the Gordian knot.

Consider the numbers.

Right after World War II, the government's debt, which reflected the huge outlays on the war effort, was 129.4 percent of the GNP, and private debt, 73.6 percent of the GNP. But then Washington, which was supposed to be spending the country into the poor house, steadily reduced that debt as a percentage of the GNP. Between 1960 and 1969, the Kennedy-Johnson years—in the dominant myth, a time of wild spending—public debt as a percentage of the GNP *fell* from 59.7 percent to 40.8 percent. At the same time, private debt rose from 112.4 percent of the GNP to 133.8 percent. And corporate reliance on short-term borrowing went up dramatically.

In 1955, short-term debt—which, according to the classic and very prudent rules, is supposed to be used for dealing with temporary cash-flow situations—was 13.5 percent of corporate product; in 1965, it was 19 percent, in 1970, 25 percent. By the late sixties, that short-term debt was almost as important a source of corporate funds as the internal savings of the corporations. After all, business participated in the Keynesian euphoria along with everyone else. If there was going to be endless growth, if the business cycle had been forever banished, then today's debts can easily be paid out of tomorrow's inevitable profits.

But when things began to go wrong in the late sixties—when profits turned out to be less than guaranteed—debt had already become a corporate habit and a constant pressure. And with the inflation of the seventies, borrowing was not simply a way of rolling over past debt; it allowed one to pay off lenders with inflated dollars that were worth less than the ones originally borrowed. American business was on its way to becoming what *Business Week*, quoting Keynes, called a "casino society" in a 1985 cover story. *Business Week* pinpointed the birth date of this phenomenon as April 26, 1973. That was the day on which an "option exchange" opened in Chicago.

The option is, of course, not a stock, but a contract enabling the holder to buy a stock within a given period at a set price. It is purchased, and traded, at a fraction of the stock's value. It is a way of allowing an individual to make a bet that the actual price will go higher than the option price, thus guaranteeing an automatic profit when the option is exercised. Now there was an organized market, not in stocks, but in options to buy stocks—the first "derivative" instrument of the new world of go-go finance. As a result, *Business Week* commented, "more and more of what transpires on the trading floors of Wall and LaSalle streets has no direct connection to the factory floors of Main Street."

The careful reader will remember that, on the very day that this pioneering step was taken in the direction of turning financial markets into a Las Vegas crapshoot, there were bankers carefully explaining to the people that workers and consumers had to content themselves with less so that the society could find the capital to meet its needs. Meanwhile, in Chicago, an ingenious new way for wasting capital had been discovered.

That trend was accentuated by the increase in paper entrepreneurship in the seventies and eighties as huge sums of borrowed money were spent on corporate takeovers—or as part of a strategy of driving up the stock prices of a threatened company and allowing the corporate raiders to realize a handsome profit when they called off their raid. That has been named "greenmail." One of the reasons Ronald Reagan's supply-side economics failed in 1982 and 1983 was precisely because so many of the tax benefits of the rich, which were supposed to fuel real-world investment and recovery, were used to play corporate games instead.

If the Left Keynesian—and Right Monetarist—interpretation is right, American business did not suddenly turn into a haven for gamblers in the late sixties, or even in April 1973. Rather, a business cycle that never did succumb to the official Keynesian policies had led to a boom in which growing corporate debt was both an inherent trend and an inflationary, destabilizing force. Like the hospital patient turned into an addict as a result of medical treatment, capital made a vice out of a necessity. This development was not *the* cause of the double-digit inflation of the seventies; but it was *a* cause, and a significant one.

Richard Nixon played a special role in this process. In his "Keynesian" phase of promoting extremely expansionist policies during 1971 and 1972, Nixon worked to get a booming economy on election day, 1972. As part of this project, he influenced Arthur Burns, then head of the Federal Reserve and the very model of a man of austere rectitude, to put the money supply at the service of his campaign. The money supply rose five and a half points between 1970 and 1971, hitting an annual rate of growth of 13.4 percent, and then remained at 13.1 percent in 1972. So political expediency joined with economic necessity in promoting the inflation of the 1970s.

This analysis also puts the OPEC price increase of 1974 into perspective. That quadrupling of energy prices is one of the most popular official Keynesian scapegoats for the collapse of the "permanent" full-employment equilibrium of the sixties. In this reading, the crisis was not a fault of the system or its policies, but of foreigners, and Arabs at that. But the fact is that, in the third quarter of 1973, *before* OPEC's action, the inflation rate had already hit 7.5 percent, which was more than double the average for the sixties. Energy prices, Edward Denison has calculated, accounted for perhaps three-tenths of a percent of the decline in growth from 1973 to 1982. They were, he wrote, "a small factor in the slowdown after 1973 but more important in the further slowdown after 1979." But the effect of the 1979 price rise seems to have been concentrated in a short period.

So there is no doubt that OPEC had an inflationary impact and that it was the most visible single cause of the price rises in 1974–75. But OPEC was not a *diabolus ex machina* and the main source of the Western crisis which pre- and postdated it. Moreover, federal spending for the poor was much less of an inflationary policy than the way in which the monetary authorities facilitated the debt habits of corporate America that were an integral part of the boom.

Conservatives like Hayek and Friedman have long insisted on this point and denounced the economic distortions resulting from cheap money as the single most important cause of our troubles. But although that analysis shares a central theme with the Left Keynesians like Robinson and Minsky, that is about all they have in common. For the conservatives deduce from that fact the necessity of going back to the equilibrium model of full employment that self-destructed in the Depression. They were, and are, for subjecting people to the miseries of joblessness in order to get the "self-regulating" economy back on an even keel.

The Left Keynesians rightly reject that call to return to the old-fashioned—and discredited—economic limits that existed before the thirties and the innovations of Roosevelt and the Swedish Socialists. And the official Keynesians desperately try to cling to the orthodoxy of the sixties, which life treated as rudely in the seventies as it did classic economics in the thirties.

VI

What does this analysis tell us about the limits that the sixties transgressed when the Great Prosperity came to an end? What does it say about the possibility of new limits in the eighties and nineties that could provide a space for both economic growth and social decency?

Clearly, one of the fundamental limits of the system—and on this point Keynes and Marx agreed, as the Swedish Socialists who synthesized them well understood—is the structure of income and wealth. That was the great problem of the Depression, when the soaring productivity of the twenties could not be absorbed by an institutionally restricted pattern of consumption. The Fordist solution was to change that structure—but not too much. There was some redistribution of the shares of income in the thirties and during World War II in the United States, but in the glory years of the boom, the rich did better than anyone else—and not accidentally, as old Henry Ford would probably have been quite happy to learn.

Even that modest change worked wonders for a while. In this country, the take-off occurred during World War II when the imperative of national defense justified a truly massive mobilization of otherwise wasted human and material resources and produced a full-employment economy with high levels of (patriotic) communal saving. In Europe, a similar process was sparked by the devastation of the war and the "socialized" investment funds that came from the United States afterward.

These trends kept their momentum as the new buying power opened up new markets for consumer durables, such as cars and television sets, and government research and development led to the emergence of a revolutionary electronics industry. But all of this took place within those rather strict Fordist limits. In its official version, Keynesianism, as John Kenneth Galbraith put it, subsidized private affluence and tolerated public squalor. That was most true in the United States and least true in the strong social democratic welfare states. But even in Sweden, the Socialist-induced boom enormously strengthened capital, and in recent years, multinational capital.

In part, this happened because of the *political* limits of Fordism. The government, as Keynes himself well understood, had to have the cooperation of the private sector in a mixed economy. To take an extreme case in point, when the Socialists in Chile under Allende tried to create a capitalist boom in order to raise up the poor and the workers, significant business elements refused to cooperate, even though they were sacrificing their own profits in the process. They simply did not want a leftist version of their system.

In the advanced capitalist economies, this political limit

meant that the Keynesian retreated from, or simply repressed, the visions of the radical Keynes of the last chapter of the *General Theory*. To put it mildly, capital was not sympathetic to the "euthanasia of the rentier." As Robert Kuttner shrewdly summarized the trend, society socialized income but without socializing wealth. Therefore, public action tended to reproduce the private maldistribution of wealth, and that was economically as well as ethically bad, for it made fiscal overload all but inevitable.

The boom of the sixties collided not with immemorial economic laws, but with the limits of an extremely moderate, corporate-oriented Keynesianism. If the next Left ignores those limits—or if it takes a "radical" stance and thinks that they are easy to transcend—it will fail. It must therefore be concerned not simply with the static inequity of the maldistribution of wealth, but with the dynamic power of elite decision making that goes with it. If it faces up to that profound challenge, then it is at least possible that there will be room for a different kind of growth through a quantum leap in justice.

Before probing that possibility, we must turn from the illusory causes of the crisis, like "crowding out," to some of the more serious reasons for the collapse of Fordism. Right now, however, we can answer the question with which we began: Did the government kill the goose that laid the golden eggs? Certainly not in the way that our myths of the sixties interpret that process. And to the extent that it did, the moral to be drawn is almost the exact opposite of the conventional wisdom. The government is responsible for the crisis because it acted in the interest of capital rather than in the interest of the vast majority of the society.

4

Causes

Major psychic events, Sigmund Freud rightly said, are "over-determined," the result of a convergence of causes, not of a single cause. So, others have added, are economic and social events.

In the last chapter, I dealt with the most popular, usually single-strand, theories of the current crisis, all of which focus on the allegedly excessive spending of government as *the* decisive factor in our predicament. In showing that matters were, and are, more complex than that, it was suggested that government spending was often the consequence of the crisis rather than its cause. Deficits soared because the unemployed receive benefits and no longer pay taxes. But why, then, was there so much joblessness in the seventies as compared to the sixties?

If the government deficits were, to some considerable degree, an effect, what were their causes?

The answer is over-determined. The new high rates of unemployment—and the crisis itself—were part of a complex transformation that affected technology and the very organization of work as well as government fiscal policy. There were social factors involved, from the relatively trivial, like new shirt styles for men, to the profound, like the sea change in the consciousness of women. So many interrelated causes were at work that I cannot neatly order them and assign them their proper rank and influence. That, however, is less a personal flaw in my analysis than an inherent structural limit in any account of an intricate spiral of change that is still in progress.

I

Technology is not technological.

Between Henry Ford's introduction of the mass-production assembly lines and the emergence of a "Fordist" system capable of coping with the enormous productivity unleashed by that innovation, thirty years intervened. They were a time of bitter class struggle and the rise of mass industrial unions, of false starts and failed solutions, such as Roosevelt's NRA. And the institutional structure that finally managed to get some kind of social control over the effects of Ford's ingenuity was that improvised, undesigned yet coherent, contraption that provided the base for the Great Prosperity. It, in turn, "determined" the meaning of the assembly line every bit as much as the assembly line determined it. The effect—and, as we will see, even the character—of technology is the work of society more than of engineers.

The failure of Fordism cannot be understood apart from the technological change that coincided with it—but it was hardly the simple determinant of that change. When the old way of producing was transformed in the sixties and seventies, it was not just the mid-twentieth century factory that became obsolete. The survival of all of the institutions that had emerged with that factory in more than half a century of stress and strain, shaping it and being shaped by it, became problematic, too.

There was no day or month or even year in which the transition took place. By the mid-fifties, there was already a marked shift away from manufacturing employment and toward the services—and yet the work force in that quintessential smokestack industry, auto, did not peak until 1979. Thus, the dramatic occupational transformation so visible in the Reagan recovery of 1982–84, when 80 percent of the new jobs were in the service sector and manufacturing employment hardly rose at all during the fastest expansion in three decades, is the culmination of a long process.

A few numbers indicate this trend. In 1972, a "good" year, there were 19.1 million workers in goods production with an output of $529.6 billion. That same year, 12.2 million were employed in the service-producing sector with a $519 billion output. In 1984, another "good" year, the goods-producing labor force had risen by a mere 400,000 but their work was worth $763.6 billion (measured in 1972 dollars). The services now employed 20.6 million men and women, but their yield was only $736.9 billion. In other words, an 8-million-plus increase in the services had added *less* new volume than the mere increment of 400,000 in goods production. Clearly a vast qualitative transformation of the economy was underway.

I cannot even begin to explore all the implications of this shift. Rather, I want to focus on the way in which the technological and occupational change subverted the institutional structure that had facilitated the golden age of the American economy in the fifties and sixties. Fordism was not simply mass-production assembly lines and a huge mass of semiskilled blue-collar workers. It was mass production plus rising wage patterns set by union members, plus governmental stimulus to further increase employment, supported by a coalition in which blue-collar labor played a key role. But the new trends created low-paid, nonunion work, and the truly massive stimulus of unprecedented annual deficits under Reagan still left more than eight million people out in the streets.

We are dealing, then, with social-economic-technological-political change, not just technological change, as one of the factors in the current crisis. This transformation was obviously not initiated by a mythically sinister government, for it was ordered from corporate boardrooms. In fact, this shift is itself a cause of government deficits in that it makes full employment more difficult and expensive to attain and thereby imposes major social costs of joblessness upon the society even at the height of a recovery.

What is the nature of the technological change involved in such a transformation of the economy? The most popular answer is "automation." That is basically right, but it is more often than not also simplistic. At times, there is even the suggestion that we are in the midst of an apocalyptic transition that will soon see the total elimination of semiskilled factory work. If we are going to make a serious analysis of the technological revolution in the world economy, it is necessary to be much more precise than a vague reference to "automation."

For instance, the huge increase in service employment in the United States in the seventies was, as Lester Thurow has shown, partly the result of cheap labor costs here, particularly for women and minorities, as compared to the situation in Europe. So evidence from the United States on the domination of the services over manufacturing is somewhat exaggerated by a factor having nothing to do with technology.

And when it comes to "automation" it is necessary to "unpack" the soaring generalizations (I follow Phil Blackburn, Rod Coombs, and Kenneth Greer in doing so). In the first period of the Industrial Revolution, there was a mechanization of the very process that *transformed* materials. In the second stage, associated with the genius of Henry Ford, the *transfer* of those materials within the factory was mechanized by the assembly line. And in the third, and present, phase, the *control* of both the transformation and transfer functions was mechanized through computers. It is this last development that alone deserves the name of "automation" (a word that Blackburn, Coombs, and Greer feel is so confused as to be useless).

In the years after World War II, there were two distinct trends working to undermine Fordism, and they are often wrongly lumped together. On the one hand, classic Fordist principles were extended throughout the manufacturing economy, and that was a source of great productivity gains. However, eventually this revolution became routine and exhausted itself, a subtle happening that we will later examine in greater detail. On the other hand, the new phase of computerized control began to accelerate that, among many other things, reshaped the social-technological structure. This development looms very large in the popular literature, largely because it is so obvious that it can be plausibly overstated.

In 1958, only 4.2 percent of machinery production in the United States was automatically controlled; in 1963, 13.9 percent; in 1972, 16.2 percent. In the critical time of the crisis of Fordism, then, the American economy was not suddenly "automated"—any more than Henry Ford's assembly line took over all of production in a few years. Both began as a technological cloud no larger than a man's hand and then proceeded toward the domination of the entire horizon. Two of the most careful students of the subject, Wassily Leontiev and Faye Duchin, put it into a historical perspective that is quite arresting. The "computer revolution," they write, will in the year 2000 "be no more advanced than the mechanization of European economies had advanced by, let us say, the year 1820"!

So the third stage of mechanization is still very much in progress. Even so, it is possible to hazard a first generalization. In the sixties and seventies, Henry Ford's assembly-line revolution lost its momentum as it was standardized throughout the entire economy at the same time that computerized controls introduced radically new methods. As a result, the mass production of huge batches of identical goods made by fixed-purpose machines run by semiskilled workers started to lose its dominant position, and there was an emergent labor force that did not know of, or mesh with, the political, economic, and social institutions that had triumphed in the Great Prosperity after World War II.

So first of all, social-technological change created a new labor force, which had both political and economic consequences.

All of this had a major, and negative, impact upon Western productivity—and upon America most of all. In being a bit more precise about this effect of social-technological change, we confront an important corollary of our opening proposition that technology is not technological: not how machines make, and unmake, social structures, which is obvious enough; but how social structures make, and unmake, the character of machines.

II

Productivity is a dangerously inexact term. In a smokestack economy, it has a relatively clear meaning, quantitatively defined by the physical output per worker employed.

But when the shift to services begins, the very concepts appropriate to Fordism no longer suffice. How does one measure the "output" of a university professor, a therapist, or a nurse's aide? To be sure, the broadest definition of the service sector includes transportation and one can construct some fairly objective indices of productivity, i.e., the increase in passenger miles per flight and flight crew as jumbo jets come on line. But my examples of occupations that make the determination of productivity problematic were not picked at random. They represent two of the major growth sectors in the expansion of service employment in the sixties and seventies: health and education. And this exceedingly unautomated trend was probably more significant in those years—when the crisis came, if not in the long run—than the industrial use of computers.

It is likely there will be yet another transformation that will change this reality. In the eighties, profit-making hospitals are working hard to "industrialize" health and, as we have seen, officials of one corporation have been making cost and profit studies of different kinds of surgery. Computers are, of course, already being used in diagnostic work as well as in the classroom where they function as infinitely patient, if inherently limited, teachers. But in the decisive years in which the crisis developed, the growth of the medical and educational components of the GNP meant a shift to labor-intensive activities that could not be organized on Fordist lines.

In the seventies, real expenses for health rose by 10.3 percent and for education by 6.1 percent. In 1960, those two sectors accounted for 4.9 percent of the GDP; in 1970, for 10 percent; and today, medicine alone takes around 10 percent of total output.

As a result, it was not just that Fordist factory methods were becoming less important; the very concepts and statistics that had described the earlier reality could hardly grasp what was happening. In his sophisticated study of productivity trends in the seventies, Edward Denison concluded that they were, to a surprising degree, a "mystery." In a later survey that covered 1929 to 1982, the most important single cause of the sharp decline in productivity that began in 1973 was, Denison wrote, a "residual" category including everything that was not explained by the standard measures.

In his analysis of the seventies, Denison noted that the old definitions no longer apply when one talks of goods-producing and service sectors "because industries or products classified in each group are completely lacking in homogeneity with respect to productivity change—or to almost anything else." What is the common measure of the efficiency of fast-food cooks, movie stars, airplane pilots, and auto workers?

Even so, Denison reports that every single economy in the West reported a significant decline in productivity starting in 1973. If I am critical of the intellectual apparatus used to quantify that fact, I am nonetheless persuaded that it is a fact. I can intuitively understand Lester Thurow's assertion that the shift to services has "been braking national productivity since World War II" because "every worker who moved into services represented a 29 percentage-point decline in productivity." Clearly it is of some moment that, in the 1970s, there were more new jobs in fast food than the total number of jobs in the steel industry. We moved, in part, at least, from the "dark, Satanic mills" to Burger King.

This growth in the non-Fordist segment of the society was, however, a consequence of Fordism itself. It is here that we begin to encounter how politics and social patterns determine the economy as well as vice versa. For one thing, the increase in health and education outlays was part of the new postwar social contract. If there was a tragic failure to create a national health system in the United States, job-related medical insurance, and then Medicare and Medicaid, were still two of the most important elements in the "socialized" wage. In Europe and Canada, where health care is largely in the public sector, this fact is even more unmistakable. And the quantum leap in education was governmentally financed throughout the West. In other words, beyond the positive impact these developments had upon health and culture—or even economics—they were the political and social preconditions of postwar growth.

Indeed, that very point was somewhat oversold in the sixties when it came to education. The "human capital" theorists said that increasing investments in high school and college would generate higher productivity, income, and tax revenues for the society as a whole. Practical people, like Lyndon Johnson, thought they had discovered a free lunch which would, moreover, turn a tidy profit for the nation. And, no question about it, the increase in schooling was one of the reasons for the extraordinary productivity of American workers in the twentieth century. Ironically, America, the most backward of the welfare states in the contemporary world, had been the first nation to adopt a universal social service, the school, and it had paid handsome dividends.

But if productivity goes up when the number of college graduates rises from 5 percent of the labor force to 10 percent, that is not necessarily true when the percentage goes from 10 percent to 20 percent, particularly if the country forgets to generate jobs that can utilize the enhanced potential of the 20 percent. That is what happened, and it led to "credentialing" in which better-trained people adapted to, rather than transformed, low-productivity jobs. In Denison's analysis, a slowing in the application of knowledge to production is one of the causes of the crisis. Perhaps that typically American hope that education alone can remake the society and thus save us from the inconvenience of serious institutional change was one reason.

And yet if the utopian dreams of the hardheaded politicians did not come to pass, the increase in employment in education—and health—did play a very practical role. It created new jobs for the poor (nurses' and teachers' aides) as well as for college graduates (teachers, professors). There was, in effect, publicly funded baby-sitting for the very young through the school and preschool system, and the arrival of more than a third of the baby-boomers on the labor market was deferred while they attended college. So educational baby-sitting—and fast and frozen foods—"freed" many women to leave unpaid work in the home and take up paid (usually low-paid) service jobs. And the second income that resulted from this trend helped families keep up with the new consumption demands of the Keynesian age.

These innovations were a fairly direct result of the political and sociological preconditions of Fordist production. Another related development was indirect and more subtle. It has to do with the evolution of taste.

As income rose because of the success of the mass production of cheap goods, the discretionary income of consumers for more expensive products also went up. Arrow Shirts was one of the first companies to discover this fact. In the late sixties, it found out that its standard products no longer satisfied the more discriminating desires of its customers. But that meant—and not just for shirts, but for automobiles and a whole range of other items—that there had to be a new system of production capable of turning out small batches of specially designed goods. And that, of course, was precisely what the mechanization of the control of production made possible. A new attitude toward shirts, itself a byproduct of Keynesian consumerism, thus made a contribution to a change in technology. The old, "gross," technology no longer sufficed.

By the seventies, there was still another spin-off from Fordist success and it collided with Fordist social policy. As the new, Keynesian generation started forming families, it began to "gentrify" the decaying sections of old cities, taking over housing that, according to our "trickle down" theory, was supposed to be occupied by the poor. Boutiques and croissant shops sprouted in working-class neighborhoods as the displacement of the blue collars in the labor force was translated into the very structures of urban life.

Two other factors affecting productivity had to do not with taste or the service sector, but with that old-fashioned bastion of Fordism itself, the plant floor. Here, too, the system turned out to be its undoing.

Productivity is social and political as well as economic, a fact that can be seen in events of the late sixties and early seventies. There "should" have been a recession in 1967 or 1968 if the normal rhythms of the business cycle had prevailed. But instead we had the war in Vietnam, with increased government spending and the beginnings of inflation rather than an economic downturn. To Lyndon Johnson's economists, that seemed proof that their policies had created a brand new economic universe in which there were no longer ups and downs. In their enthusiasm over the good news, they ignored the fact that the economy had not only skipped the unhappiness of a recession but had been deprived of its normal function as well.

For recessions are not simply breakdowns in the system; they are functional breakdowns that cruelly prepare the way for a new economic advance. When unemployment rises, trade unionists accept very moderate wage increases and discipline in the factory shapes up. The workers are brutally reminded that they should be thankful to have a job—any job—rather than being out on the street. In the late sixties, that didn't happen. One consequence was that labor demanded, and often got, more money; another was that workers began to concern themselves not simply with money, but with the conditions of working life as well.

The strike of a relatively young work force at the Lordstown, Ohio, plant of General Motors caught the public's imagination. Here were trade unionists becoming militant about the speed of the assembly line and the quality of their lives on the job. But the essence of Fordism was to maintain a quasi-military discipline in the shop and, above all, to submit everything to the imperatives of the assembly line. So management endured this indiscipline, which sapped the very sources of Fordist productivity only so long.

The phenomenon was international, extending throughout the advanced capitalist world. That is what very strongly suggests that it is a systemic feature of the Fordist system itself at a certain point in its development. There was May 1968 in France which saw not simply student barricades in the Latin Quarter but a general strike of the working class as well. In Italy there was the "Hot Autumn" of 1969; in West Germany, an unprecedented strike wave. Three specialists, Robert J. Flanagan, David W. Soskice, and Lloyd Ulman, wrote that "the waves of industrial conflict in Western European countries in the late 1960s were not coincidental." Here, too, a pent-up working-class response to rationalization plus an employer reaction to reduced profitability and the appearance of inflation played a role.

In the seventies in Italy, for instance, women had won the right in some plants to study feminism and politics on company time. Luciana Castelina, an Italian Marxist, remembers that it was almost impossible to fire a worker. In the United States, the labor struggle was not as radical as it was in Italy and the France of 1968—and yet black workers in Detroit did form "revolutionary" auto unions in the late sixties. Indeed, in both the United States and Europe, strata that had previously played little or no role in the workers' movement, either because they were marginal to it or totally absent from it—women, minorities, uprooted peasants—often turned into militant forces.

The possibility of these trends was the result of Fordist success. Expansion, near full employment, the lure of more and more profits—all made workers a scarce, and therefore powerful, resource. Management did not sit idly by.

In the early seventies—when, Denison holds, the decisive decline in productivity began—there was a counteroffensive from the front office. But if the relatively high employment of the late sixties had inspired worker resistance to speed-up and other hallowed Fordist customs, now there was hostility on the shop floor to management's "get tough" drive. Productivity had become problematic because of the way in which a "missed" recession and excessively good times emboldened the workers; now it went down as angry men and women fought back against a renewed meanness on the part of capital.

Finally, there was a subtle factor at work on the assembly line itself. Back in the nineteenth century, capital had already sought to mechanize production as a means of reducing the discretion—and thus the social and economic power—of the workers as far as possible. As Harry Braverman described the process in his classic study, *Labor and Monopoly Capital*, labor was systematically "deskilled" over time. Fordism made that trend scientific and systematic. By mechanizing the transfer of materials within the plant, it eliminated those potential bottlenecks that had previously been controlled by human beings who gained some strategy power as a result. More recently, industrial computerization has been carried out with the explicit intention of excluding men and women from the production process.

In assembly-line industry, there was—and still is—a secret war between workers and management over the fruits of knowledge. When someone on the line figures out a way to perform a job more efficiently than the company, he or she hoards that information, concealing it from the foreman, using it in order to snatch a few minutes of freedom from the compulsion of the system. And the company, for its part, is always trying to figure out better ways of programming people and machines to do things the "one best way"—the company's way.

The corporations won that war; the workers achieved only brief, guerrilla victories. But eventually that drive to incorporate the knowledge and skills of human beings into machines ran into absolute limits. For one thing, Fordism was extended to every nook and cranny of the economy and there were no more traditional inefficiencies left to conquer. For another, there came a point when there was little left to expropriate from the skill of the workers. A vein of productivity had been exhausted at the same time that the new, much more flexible technology and the needs for speciality products actually forced the companies to reskill their workers.

Each case outlined in this section—the shift to the service sector, the militancy of the late sixties and then the anger of the early seventies, the end of a major source of productivity gains—was the result, or precondition, of Fordist success. So was a massive change in class structure.

III

These trends have opened the way to the "society of three speeds," with a privileged elite, a downgraded middle, and a permanently precarious bottom. This constellation might even mean, in the eighties or nineties, the return of some of the problems of the 1920s.

Fordism, we have noted, created its own distinctive class

structure centered upon that mass of semiskilled workers who tended the fixed-purpose, high-productivity machines. In 1950, more than 41 percent of the labor force were craftspeople, operatives, and laborers, and another 11.8 percent were farm laborers. The professional and technical stratum accounted for 8.6 percent. By 1982, nonagricultural workers of all kinds were down to 30 percent, the farm laborers were a mere 2.7 percent of the total—but the professional and technical category had doubled, to 16.3 percent. Indeed, there were now more professionals than factory workers.

This momentous transition is not simply sociological. It is political in that it has contracted the mass political base of the old New Deal coalition. It is economic in that the relatively high wages that union labor received provided a mass-consumption market for the mass-production goods it produced. It is social and cultural in that the raw numbers conceal the fact that most women and minorities who entered the work force in the seventies landed in low-paying service jobs rather than in factories, thus reinforcing racial and gender discrimination. And it was international even within the borders of the United States because of the presence of an enormous, but uncounted, number of undocumented workers who toiled in menial—and even sweatshop—jobs.

These developments were greeted by a relentless, Panglossian optimism on the part of the mainstream liberals and conservatives. A 1984 study by the Business Roundtable, an organization of the corporate elite, cited a stable percentage of manufacture in GNP to show that there was little to worry about. Charles Schultze, the chairman of the Council of Economic Advisors under President Carter and a leader of the traditional liberals at Brookings, said that proposals for an industrial policy were "a dangerous solution to an imaginary problem." And so on. The most popular—"realist"—argument for complacency was usually preceded by a quotation from Joseph Schumpeter on the virtue of "creative destruction" in a capitalist economy. Having made that obeisance, a 1984 New York Stock Exchange study then commented, "Yes, it is definitely true that more lower-paying jobs than higher-paying jobs will be generated in the coming years; many more custodial jobs will open up in the future than will computer technician jobs—for a very good reason: There has always been and probably will always be more people working in the lower-skill, lower-income jobs than in higher-skill, higher-income jobs." The Stock Exchange, not so incidentally, thus forgot the critical experience of Fordism that had seen a vast upgrading of the work force.

But the master argument for optimism was almost always taken from the transition from the horse and buggy to the automobile. Wouldn't it have been insane, one is asked, to "protect" the buggy makers and retard the development of the car, a transformation that ultimately created infinitely more jobs than any attempt at enforced stagnation would have done? That is the exact opposite error to the one committed by the New York Stock Exchange: Rather than forgetting Fordism it assumes that it is an eternal option. It is true that once the economic, social, and political institutions were in place to contain Ford's innovation, the automobile had a wondrous effect on the labor force, creating millions of new openings for displaced buggy makers and, for that matter, for the hordes of farmers who came to the city during that period.

But the transition we now face occurs precisely at the moment of the *decline* of Fordism and the disappearance of those smokestack jobs. It is conceivable that someday in the misty future a benign providence will provide a substitute for that factory work, but in the real world, during the past decade or so, it has not. What is now happening is that the percentage of manufacture is indeed relatively stable, just as the Panglosses say, but without any serious increase in manufacturing jobs at a time when the service sector is taking off.

In 1984, a Department of Labor analysis showed that, of more than five million workers who had seen their jobs eliminated (not temporarily closed down, but abolished) over a four-year period, the majority had either been driven from the labor force, were still unemployed, or had found new work at significantly lower pay. So it is that part-time work, sweatshops, and "homework"— three forms of extreme exploitation in the early period of industrialism—have returned in the age of the computer.

If, Leontiev and Duchin concluded in their input-output projections of the labor market, maximum computerization takes place between now and the year 2000, but without any new breakthroughs, there will be a loss of more than twenty million jobs in the United States compared to what would have happened if the 1978 technological mix had prevailed. Moreover, they also note that since 1960, the labor input in the production of computers has been going down, ironically because mass production methods are at work. The equipment that is fabricating a post-Fordist environment is often made by Fordist techniques.

There is not going to be an apocalyptic transition to a workerless economy or, in all likelihood, to Depression levels of mass unemployment (even though that latter possibility cannot be totally discounted). But the trend is already underway toward the "society of three speeds" that could be so vividly glimpsed in the recovery from the 1982 recession. The upper stratum—the wealthy, the professionals, and the technicians—did very well; the middle stratum saw its real wages pushed down; and even though there was the most rapid growth in thirty years, both unemployment and poverty persisted at rates previously associated with bad times. Soup kitchens and makeshift housing proliferated at the same time as former slums were gentrified and a new market for home computers boomed.

I find these events an affront to moral values, but that is not my central point here. In terms of the future of the American economy—of the fate of the privileged as well as that of the precarious—the tendency is ominous. In the 1920s there was a technological explosion, but wages did not keep pace with it, union organization declined, and a popular book celebrated Jesus Christ as the prototype of an entrepreneur. There was also a speculative frenzy, which might well be echoed in the "casino society" of the seventies and eighties, and a credit structure that has its analogies to the present situation. Eventually, of course, there was the Crash: first the collapse of the speculative house of cards, then layoffs in small business and trade, and finally mass unemployment in the gigantic plants whose capacity could not be absorbed by a socially mean society.

Is this to say that 1929 is at hand? Not necessarily and even not very likely. But it is to argue that there are new tendencies toward underconsumption that arise as the result of the occupational shift, the consequence of the end of Fordism. Defense spending, skyrocketing consumer debt, enormous tax relief for the upper classes and the corporations, and the expansion of the computer and croissant sectors can fuel a recovery, as happened in 1983 and 1984, particularly when foreign investors provide a substantial portion of the cash. But that success further subverts the most fundamental single cause of the Great Prosperity: the socialized mass consumption that made private mass production economically possible.

In 1985, the savings of the American people fell to the lowest level (as a percentage of disposable income) ever. At the same time, those nonsavers borrowed more and more money to keep a consumption-led recovery limping along. And union wage settlements fell a bit behind the low increases in the inflation rate. Those short-run developments understandably worried sophisticated business people as well as social critics. But if they looked at the deeper trends—at the way in which the evolution of the class structure had the potential for contracting consumer markets and thereby undoing the Fordist solution of the Great Prosperity—they would have been even more disturbed.

IV

The greatest single beneficiary of Fordism, private corporate capital, was also a victim of its triumph.

The idea of an "overaccumulation" of capital is at least as old as Karl Marx's *Das Kapital*. That same process that led to the higher wages and militancy described in the last section had a negative impact on business. For, all things being equal, profits went down when the wages went up, and this explains why the crisis almost always breaks out at the very height of the boom. Capitalism, Marx said, cannot tolerate the conditions that capitalist success creates—there is an "overaccumulation of capital," too much of a good thing—and it is at that point that the system needs the purgation of a recession. In the sixties, there were some distinctively modern additions to this classic scenario. In effect, government policy made the problematic tendencies in Marx's free-market model even more pronounced.

During the early and mid-sixties, there was that enormous "supply-side" surge in investment that was handsomely subsidized by Washington. The 1966 report of Lyndon Johnson's Council of Economic Advisors entitled one section (in capital letters), "KEY ROLE OF BUSINESS FIXED INVESTMENT." Investment, the liberal economists proudly asserted, had surged at a rate twice as fast as the growth of the GNP itself. The reasons for that remarkable development, the report continued, included "the investment tax credit, the liberalized depreciation rules, and the lowered corporate income tax rates." It was this government-sponsored investment that led to the higher productivity which was the key to simultaneous higher profits and higher wages.

But there was a sorcerer's apprentice at work in this idyll and one can glimpse it first of all in the growing outlays for depreciation. In the decade of the sixties, they rose by almost 45 percent; by 1980, they were more than twice as high as in 1960 (measured in constant dollars). From a corporate point of view, the good news was that Washington's treatment of depreciation was based on a legal fiction designed, precisely, to put more money in business's investment funds. And the bad news was that, in an extremely dynamic economy, much of the value of existing assets was being destroyed as new methods and plants rendered them obsolete. Management always displays a Buddhist tolerance for necessity when Schumpeter's process of "creative destruction" strikes at workers. Now that fate was attacking capital itself.

The marvelous gains in productivity that undermined the worth of pre-existing investments were quite bearable during the glory years since they brought the profits that more than compensated for the loss. But when those productivity gains slowed in the late sixties, the underpinnings of the system were shaken, particularly because, for a time at least, wages did not go down. So companies had to borrow to cover the inherited cost of the devaluation visited upon them by their own remarkable accomplishments. The huge rise in corporate debt was not simply, as noted, a result of the profit drive remaining vigorous even when the internal resources to fund it were no longer plentiful. Now, how could one balance the books when it was necessary to write off assets whose value had been destroyed by the very success of the corporation? There was, in short, a new—"socialized"—version of that old-fashioned crisis, the overaccumulation of capital.

Inflation was not a conscious corporate plot to deal with this situation—that implies a brilliance and capacity for control on the part of the business elite that simply does not exist—but it certainly helped. If one wrote those losses off in inflated dollars, it was not so painful. Indeed, one can argue that inflation was, in fact, if not by design, the substitute for the missed recession of the late sixties. One of the many ways in which a recession copes with the problems of success is that it drives out the inefficient competitors and allows the strong corporations to close down their obsolete, or not so profitable, plants and, by thus cruelly devaluing old investments, makes new investments once more desirable. Inflation did that, too, but in a new and disturbing way.

The problem was that, in so far as depreciation was a real-world process and not simply a device for lowering taxes owed to the government, the corporations now had to replace their obsolete plant at much higher prices than they had ever anticipated. Throughout the seventies, business complained loud and long that it was being driven to the poorhouse by this very process—without adding that the dynamic that had created the situation was the product of government subsidies gladly accepted by the private sector and of . . . the sixties boom itself.

The resulting schizophrenia was dramatized by an article in *Business Week* at the height of inflation. Corporations were complaining that their profits were being artificially increased because of gains on inventories (in a time of rapidly rising prices, simply holding goods makes money) and that they suffered from the concealed losses that came from a devaluation of their assets which was no longer covered by the (pre- or lower-inflation) depreciation allowances. Fine, *Business Week* replied. A company can get a more realistic picture of its position simply by changing its accounting system to recognize these trends. The problem was, that would make profits go down and turn away investors. The private sector wanted the legerdemain of inflation—and it hated it. That, of course, is the way it feels about a recession and its functional destructiveness. The new way of coping with the excessive success of the system was as contradictory as the old.

Keynes, it will be remembered, predicted troubles of this sort if his ideas were ever applied. His disciples ignored his warnings and, if they even knew of the analysis of the overaccumulation of capital, regarded it as a nineteenth-century curiosity. Reality, however, did a stunning imitation of theory.

V

Have I created a perfect alibi for the welfare state? If government spending was not the main culprit, and the basic problem was that the system, in a thousand ways, eventually could not abide its government-induced triumph, was social policy then a totally innocent victim of forces beyond its control?

Of course not. But before it was possible to confront the real difficulties of the welfare state, it was necessary to deal with the reactionary and mythological attacks upon it. That done, we can now turn to the problems caused by increases in the simple humanity of capitalism during the postwar years. If it was not their "fault" that the system could not tolerate them very well, it still was a fact.

Entitlements, such as AFDC, food stamps, and unemployment compensation, increased even when the political mood shifted to the right. They are all automatically increased by a crisis and that is one of the many reasons why, in the late seventies and early eighties, a one-point rise in joblessness added $30 billion to the deficit. The indexing of social security was a device to pass inflation through the most massive single domestic expenditure of the government *and* a totally necessary defense of vulnerable people.

To be sure, the primary fault is not to be found in the welfare state. Had the Keynesian expectations of the sixties, which were the basis of many of these open-ended social commitments, been fulfilled, they would not have been a problem at all. Indeed, they would have enlarged markets, just as in the good old days. It was the slowdown in productivity and growth that created difficulties, not the minimal measures that dealt with some of the cruelest consequences of that economic failure. But once the process was underway, and particularly in the mid-seventies when all Western governments tried to deal with a radical new situation without turning on the poor, there was an inherited social cost that made the control of the malfunctioning economy even more of a problem.

There is an extremely important and related problem and it bears very much upon the future: the way in which many of those social benefits are financed. In every Western country—and in France above all—"payroll taxes" play an important role. They require the employer to pay a certain percentage of the insurance cost of various programs. But that acts, as François Mitterrand discovered, to discourage hiring. And when times get bad it motivates employers to take on part-time help not covered by the payroll taxes—or to have recourse to an underground economy that is not taxed at all. Pierre Rosanvallon argues, with some justice, that the emergence of the underground economy is, among many other things, a form of protest against the tax cost of doing business in the welfare state.

What conclusion does one draw from the trend? To turn against social decency in the name of efficiency? I think not. The proper response is *to search for other ways to finance social decency*, ways that will not act as employment disincentives. The French economist Serge Christophe Kolm has persuasively said that governments of the Left should not try to improve the living standard of the poor by rapidly increasing their wages and payroll tax benefits. Rather, leave the production process alone and then tax income and wealth in a redistributive fashion after the fact. Obviously such taxes can eventually become a disincentive, a point to which we will return. But they are not the immediate discouragement to hiring that payroll taxes are.

More broadly, there is a current of Left-Right criticism of the welfare state that takes it to task for its bureaucratic qualities.

Unfortunately, this legitimate concern for the rights and sensibilities of the poor often gets mixed up with a reactionary myth: that the leviathan state has grown enormously under the impact of Fordism. In the United States, the number of civilian employees of the federal government hardly increased at all during the sixties and seventies. The new social jobs were created, precisely, at the state and local levels that are the apple of the conservative eye. And throughout the West in the postwar period, direct government consumption—where the choices are made by those sinister bureaucrats—rose by 40.7 percent while "socially financed private consumption" went up by 106.8 percent. Most of the expenditures, then, supported free choice in the capitalist market.

But if the myths about the welfare state are false, the fact remains that the Fordist solution involved a considerable bureaucratization of social life. A neoconservative like Nathan Glazer says much the same thing as a near-anarchist radical like Ivan Illich: that government social conscience has undercut the home, the neighborhood, the church—those primordial "public affections" of which Edmund Burke spoke. The problem is, the neoconservatives yearn to go back to a past that has been irrevocably destroyed by the urbanization and industrialization of the capitalist dynamic. Still, their critique will point us, when it comes to alternatives, toward decentralized and voluntarist social programs.

Finally, one of the most profound analyses of the contradictions of the welfare state has come from the Left, particularly from the Marxist sociologist Claus Offe. There were, Offe suggests, two master trends in the years of Fordist success, and the government supported both, even though they contradicted one another.

On the one hand, those years saw a relentless commercialization of every aspect of social life.

This was most obvious in the case of the radical redefinition of the role of women in the society. One way to stimulate economic growth is to bring whole new strata into the labor force: women; underemployed agricultural laborers and small, or subsistence, farmers; minorities; foreigners; and, in Europe, uprooted peasants. That provides a labor force that, not yet socialized to the demands of unionized workers, is willing to undertake menial jobs. It is, for instance, of some moment that there was no Western society in the seventies in which males from the dominant ethnic group(s) did the "dirty work."

This has obvious advantages from a corporate point of view—but it transforms social relations at the same time. The nature of the family is changed as more and more women enter the paid labor force; the family farms disappear; the state takes over the financial responsibility for, and often the care of, the aging; an increasingly multiracial working class is segmented in ways that institutionalizes discrimination against minorities, undocumented workers, or "guest workers." There is, in short, a considerable social cost, psychological as well as economic, in this transition, and the welfare state must deal with it.

Why do all these new strata submit to the imperious logic of commercialization? For economic reasons. It has been clearly established, for instance, that most of the women who came into the U.S. job market in the sixties and seventies did so, not so much in search of personal liberation, but because later marriage trends meant they were single and self-supporting for a longer time, and then marriage itself demanded two incomes under Keynesian standards of consumption. The "Malthusian" element in society—who does not work shall not eat—was reinforced in a way that Malthus never would have imagined.

At the same time, there was the opposite trend: the decommercialization of more and more areas of life.

In order to socialize a part of the wage and deal with the economic problem of underconsumption, individuals had to be protected against some of the more vicious Malthusian constraints. There were social security, socialized health (everywhere but in the United States), unemployment insurance, a massive increase in public funds for education, and so on. The culture was, in a sense, becoming schizophrenic, simultaneously more and less commercial. And this, as we have seen in the case of the abuse of welfare-state rights in Europe, sometimes led the welfare state to the worst of both capitalism and socialism.

Yet, there was another, extremely positive, consequence of

these trends, even though it was indeed problematic for the established order. The new strata drawn into the booming economy also discovered their own sense of dignity and sometimes became militant when they realized that the soaring promises of the Great Prosperity were not really meant for them. That was clearly a significant source of the insurgency of minorities, women, and students in the sixties and seventies.

That also meant that there were social as well as economic reasons behind the drive for "discipline" that motivated so many corporate and political leaders in the seventies. In a famous interview on the day after his landslide victory in 1972, Richard Nixon denounced all of the problems of the nation, from the smoking of marijuana to the failures of the economy, as a consequence of the liberal permissiveness of the sixties. That was reactionary nonsense based, as such nonsense usually is, on a kernel of truth. The Great Prosperity did indeed loosen many of the traditional bonds, and it is even right to talk of a spiritual crisis that occurred as a result. But there is no way back to the traditional values in a totally untraditional society. What is needed is a new social and individual morality.

It turned out that those most unlikely cothinkers Henry Ford and Antonio Gramsci had understood something basic more than half a century ago: that the economic changes wrought by Fordism would remake the social and psychological structure of the West as well as its factories. That development, too, was part of the crisis.

VI

Finally, the crisis of Fordism was, and is, international.

In some ways that is ironic, for the system was, in the period after World War II, inward looking, national, not global. During those years most of the advanced countries were engaged in expanding their own mass-consumption base so as to be able to contain their prodigies of production. Then, in complete violation of Lenin's theory of imperialism, the advanced capitalisms began to invest more in each other's affluence and less in the poverty of the Third World.

In the first phase of the Great Prosperity, say from 1945 to the late sixties, the United States was so totally dominant that it was able to give a coherence to the world capitalist market. The globe observed a dollar standard, a tribute to the fact that the war-devastated economies could not get enough American goods or the currency that represented them. The Marshall Plan and related efforts functioned as a kind of international Keynesianism, but only for potentially rich nations. Washington gave money, or lent it at concessionary rates, to the Europeans and Japanese who then turned around and spent the money in the United States. Internationalism was profitable—which is not to say that making money was the motive for it, but simply that the fact made compassion, decency, and cold-war anticommunism quite affordable.

At Bretton Woods that hegemonic American position was institutionalized. There was, however, a very interesting conflict between the United States, represented by Harry Dexter White, and Britain, in the person of Keynes himself. Keynes wanted to create a truly international currency—called "Bancor"—and to relate it to a global notion of full employment. The United States, which was after all the linchpin of the entire system, did not want control of credit to escape from its own hands in this fashion. And given the economic and political realities of the period, the resolution of the debate was foreordained: The United States won.

But then a number of things happened, all of which eventually contributed to the crisis of the seventies. The postwar effort at reconstructing the advanced capitalism worked too well as the European and Japanese clients of the late forties and the fifties turned into the competitors of the sixties. The multinational corporation began its progress toward the domination of one-third of the world product, and national Fordism lost control over some of its most important institutions—a fact that François Mitterrand was to learn about to his extreme sorrow.

These shifts, plus the approaching crisis of Fordism itself and the economic impact of the American war in Vietnam, led to a basic turning point in 1971 when Richard Nixon unilaterally put an end to the Bretton Woods system and world currencies began to "float." There was thus a new instability at work around the globe: In the late seventies, Europeans were outraged that the dollar was so egregiously undervalued; in the eighties they were furious that it was so egregiously overvalued.

These trends, it must be noted, were in motion *before* the OPEC price increases of 1974–75. They were aggravated by that development, to be sure, but not caused by it. And indeed, that OPEC move led to what was first seen as a triumph of the Western banking system. There was, in effect, a new "Marshall Plan," particularly for Latin America, as banks in the United States recycled petrodollars from the oil producers, lending them to Third World countries for development (Latin America in particular) and, in the case of those without oil, such as Brazil, to pay for their new energy costs. Once again it seemed that everyone was winning.

But then came the chronic inflation of the seventies and the second oil shock of 1979, and those same countries now saw their debts soar to intolerable levels. The combination of the end of Bretton Woods, OPEC, the shortsightedness of the American banks, and double-digit inflation had brought the world economic system to the point where a major financial collapse was possible. It still is.

During the seventies, there was also a tremendously important misunderstanding between the North and the South. In the United Nations, the poor countries presented proposals for a "New International Economic Order" (NIEO) which were couched in radical, even revolutionary, rhetoric but were rather moderate, and quite capitalist, in content. The idea of stabilizing raw-material prices by means of an international fund that would support prices when they fell to a certain level, and then recoup its losses by selling its holdings when they rose again, should have been familiar to Americans. It was a global application of the agricultural support system that had been operating for years within the United States.

But the major Western powers saw NIEO as a dangerous attempt at global redistribution and, after a brief flirtation with the idea out of fear that the OPEC cartel might be replicated for other essential materials, turned away from even thinking about it. So when the crisis hit in the late seventies, and particularly after the second oil shock, there was a kind of international economic anarchy within the advanced countries and between them and the developing nations. But at the same time that the institutions of international control were crumbling, international economic activity became all the more integrated through the multinationals.

These, in briefest possible compass, are just a few of the global elements at work in the crisis of Fordism.

VII

The data simply do not support the monocausal notion that it was government spending that was primarily responsible for killing the goose that laid the golden eggs of the Great Prosperity. There is a further corroboration of the complexity of our plight, for it is clear that the origins of our problems are to be found on the plant floor, in the evolution of taste, in the psyches of minorities and women and ex-peasants, and in the international economy as well as in the halls of government. We are living through a social-economic-political-cultural-technological upheaval. To trivialize that historic transition in a devil theory is dangerous, even if it might help win an election or two.

If this analysis is correct, then two rather radical propositions follow: that the crisis is, in the mid-eighties, far from over; and that the solutions must be as multifaceted as the problems they confront.

5

Keynesianism for the Rich

The economic policies of Ronald Reagan's first administration were contradictory, even incoherent, but achieved a temporary success through what the London *Economist* called "Keynesianism by mistake." And yet, there was a consistency in everything Reagan did, whether he knew it or not: He made the system profitable again by attacking the social wage that had been the basis of the Great Prosperity. That was the main cause of his triumph and it will be the prime source of the downfall of his unrevolutionary revolution.

Reagan was an expansionist: He put through a deep tax cut and threw money at military problems in a bold and ineffective way that made the social spending of the sixties liberals pale by comparison. Reagan was a deflationist: He cheered monetary policies that brought the highest interest rates in the century and forced the auto and housing industries to their knees. When a recovery came, the president, an inspired political practitioner of the fallacy *post hoc, ergo propter hoc*—what comes before must be the cause of what comes after, the rain is the result of the rain dance—claimed a totally unearned vindication and convinced a majority of the voters that he deserved credit for what took place in spite of his policies.

I will be somewhat more analytic than Mr. Reagan, though that is hard when exploring a dynamic contradiction. The central point is clear enough: that the attack on the social wage did indeed resolve some of the problems of Fordism *and* has prepared the way for a structural crisis in the not too distant future.

I

We must never forget that, as I have pointed out, Ronald Reagan was the radical candidate in the 1980 election. Jimmy Carter, who had moved from a timid liberalism in 1977 to a timid conservatism in 1979, was the champion of an exhausted status quo.

Reagan was not a radical in the traditional rightist sense of the word, a free market absolutist. In that definition, the New Deal and all of its successor liberalisms had been impossibilities from the very start. When those famous eternal economic laws finally took their revenge on Roosevelt and his heirs, and the conservatives came to power, they would follow an austere and virtuous path, disdaining cheap money and irresponsible subsidies, once again allowing supply and demand to regulate the economy instead of politicians.

That was the message of the Goldwater campaign of 1964 and of Reagan's unsuccessful bid for the nomination in 1976. And even after the 1976 election, the traditional conservative—and former chairman of the Council of Economic Advisors—Herbert Stein recounts, Reagan told his friends that the transition from left to right would require a big "bellyache" of unemployment and recession. This was the classic radicalism of the Right, a principled rejection of Fordism and all of its works, a trumpet call to retreat to pre-Keynesian policies.

The Ronald Reagan who won the presidency in 1980 had broken decisively with that old conservative radicalism, and so had most, but by no means all, of the Republican Party. Reagan had given up austerity. He was now the preacher of what Herbert Stein contemptuously calls "the economics of joy," a bizarre anti-welfare-state Keynesianism for the rich that was a daring—and, as it turned out, utterly flawed—departure from the conventional wisdom of both the Right and Left as it had been defined for a half-century.

Richard Nixon, it will be remembered, was the last successful Keynesian before Reagan, promoting his landslide victory in 1972 through a fiscal and monetary expansion that made a major contribution to inflation in the seventies. It was immediately after that triumph that Nixon veered sharply back to the right. This was the period when Republican theorists discovered a capital shortage that had been caused by the profligacy of the Kennedy-Johnson years. The government had killed the goose that laid the golden eggs by "crowding" private business out of financial markets as Washington sopped up savings to pay for the debilitating benefits of the Great Society.

That charge, we have seen, was false. But there was a subordinate theme in the capital-shortage campaign that related very much to the real world. We were, it was said, becoming uncompetitive in the global market because of those mistaken liberal policies. The problem was quite real, the analysis of it quite wrong.

The postwar reconstruction of Europe and Japan had succeeded all too well. Suddenly there were competitors where once there had been grateful clients lined up to buy American goods with Marshall Plan dollars. The tremendous increase in postwar trade, so vigorously pushed by Washington, had now turned into a threat. Export and import percentages doubled in the United States during the decade of the seventies.

This country, which had been more independent of the rest of the planet than any other advanced nation, suddenly became open to foreign penetration to a degree it had never known before.

That trend was, of course, exacerbated by the emergence of the multinational corporation after the war. By producing goods in various countries around the globe, it eluded national fiscal and monetary control and eventually undercut a good part of the older Keynesian wisdom. Indeed, by the eighties, two-thirds of world trade took place between the subsidiaries of the multinationals rather than on the open market. And the automobile industry, that original and quintessential Fordist sector, saw the cozy world of administered prices and gas-guzzling cars invaded by efficient foreign competitors with energy-saving vehicles.

When there are new environmental regulations, the saying goes, the Japanese hire a hundred more engineers, the Americans a hundred more lawyers. To which one could add in the seventies: a hundred more lawyers and fifty advertising account executives to blame welfare-state spending for the international consequences of policies that had subsidized business at home and abroad during the years of economic growth.

Under these circumstances, it became a Republican commonplace to argue that there had to be less social spending in order to promote greater private investment and a new burst of productivity and international competitiveness. But at the same time that the mainstream Right was repeating this conservative "true faith," the new radicalism was taking shape. It was being developed by two economists, Arthur Laffer and Robert Mundell, by a very effective publicist, Jude Wanniski, an editorial writer for the *Wall Street Journal*, and by a somewhat maverick Republican congressman, Jack Kemp of Buffalo, New York.

The core idea of this new radicalism was succinctly formulated by George Gilder in his book *Wealth and Poverty*, one of the most influential volumes of the first Reagan administration. Gilder wrote, "There is indeed such a thing as a free lunch." It would be hard to imagine a description better designed to outrage traditional Republican conservatives. They had been attacking the welfare-staters for years on the grounds that the latter believed in a "free lunch." In fact, the Right repeated like a prayer, anything that purports to be free, like the snacks that used to be provided by taverns (the original "free lunch") or welfare checks, was covertly charged to someone. It was incorporated in the higher price for beer in the tavern, which discriminated against those who didn't like the snacks, or in the higher taxes to cover the costs of welfare checks.

The free-lunch adage was *the* popular wisdom of American conservatism for half a century. Now it was being rejected in the name of . . . conservatism. Gilder and the supply-siders argued that there was a tremendous reservoir of wasted wealth in the American economy because the tax system created disincentives for both work and investment. Lower the tax rate, they continued, and people would voluntarily work harder and invest more and thereby serve the nation a free lunch. Even though the initial impact of the tax cuts might be a loss in federal revenue and an increase in the deficit, in the not very long run the tax reductions would more than pay for themselves as surging growth would put the national accounts into the black.

These tax cuts were, their proponents said, not designed according to the despised principles of "demand-side" stimulation, i.e., through putting money into people's pockets in order to get the economy moving. That was the problem, not the solution, for it gave consumption the priority over production. Now, the "supply-side" reductions would be oriented toward encouraging more savings and investment. To do that—and this undiplomatic point was made before congressional committees rather than on the stump—tax policy had to discriminate in favor of the rich. After all, the working people and the middle class would primarily consume their tax savings; only those who had more than enough would utilize their windfall to build up the supply side.

So the first incarnation of supply-side economics, the Kemp-Roth bill of 1977, called for an "across the board" reduction of $100 billion in tax levies over three years. That is a seemingly "fair" way of giving the rich more, since a 10 percent tax reduction for the wealthy is worth much more than it is for an auto worker. By 1978, the Republican National Committee had approved Kemp-Roth—and Ronald Reagan followed suit with his usual enthusiasm.

So it was that a perverse Keynesianism, based on an anti-welfare state analysis and systematically biased toward the upper classes, was put into place. There was yet another departure from the classic conservative doctrine and it was to have significant consequences. When the capital-shortage argument was developed in the mid-seventies, there were all kinds of estimates—from William Simon, then secretary of the treasury, the New York Stock Exchange, the Chase Manhattan Bank—on how much money "should" be invested in the economy. That is, of course, a planner's concept. For a market economist, the amount of money that "should" be put into the economy is determined by supply and demand. If the supply of capital is low and interest rates are high, that is a sign that the market had decided, in its mysterious infallibility, that more investments should not be made.

Keynes had, in his own way, insisted on a corollary of that classic point. It was not, he said, the willingness of workers to work for much less, or the availability of capital, that caused business to invest, but the prospect of making a profit off the investment. Workers and money were cheap and abundant in the depths of the Depression and there were no takers. But the supply-siders had forgotten this basic characteristic of a profit motive they otherwise exalted: that business decisions are motivated by the expectation of making money. Events were to prove this strange error a fatal flaw.

It would, of course, be absurd to suggest that Ronald Reagan won the 1980 election because the public understood, and voted for, his new, radical theory. Average citizens were probably swayed by the candidate's telling them that they would receive a very large tax cut. Appreciating such a promise did not require that one grasp the Laffer Curve. And Reagan also preached standard conservative themes: family, work, neighborhood, peace, and freedom. It was not at all apparent that he was the proponent of the government carrying out an audacious experiment on the economy based on an unproved theory, i.e., that he was more of a social engineer than any liberal politician had ever been.

In David Stockman's *The Triumph of Politics*, there is an incredible account of how abstract and unworldly—how utterly ideological—the Reagan administration was when it tried to follow the true doctrine. It was necessary for the White House to forecast the development of the economy as a basis for calculating its various proposals. The supply-siders, Stockman tells us, wanted a very high figure for real growth in GNP because that would prove that their own schemes had worked. But the monetarists wanted a very low "in money" GNP (real GNP plus the rate of inflation) to show that their own nostrums had held prices down. So they simply asserted that what would have to happen to make their contradictory policies come true would in fact happen. The Reagan planners had entered fantasyland, and it turned out that every one of their "predictions" failed.

But when it came to political practice, Reagan was as good as his word in one important policy area: The tax burden was indeed shifted from the rich to the poor, the working people, and the middle class. Since everyone, except the poor, got *something*, most people did not realize that their relative burden had been raised even as their taxes declined. A study by the Urban Institute—there are prominent Republicans as well as Democrats on its board—showed that, between 1980 and 1984, the bottom 20 percent of the population suffered a 7.6 percent decrease in its disposable personal income. The next 20 percent went down by 1.7 percent, the middle fifth went up by a mere .9 of 1 percent, while the fourth quintile gained 3.4 percent and the top 20 percent increased their income by 8.7 percent.

That might seem to be a mere statistical abstraction. Yet in explaining why the percentage of the poor who are children has risen dramatically in recent years, the bipartisan Congressional Research Search concluded that one major reason was the growth in inequality in the United States. In 1968, the top fifth had 4.6 times the income of the bottom fifth; in 1983, its share was 8 times greater, and the poor had become poorer, the children above all. A good part of this trend came from Reagan's attack on the social wage.

So it was that the administration gave households with incomes of $80,000 a year or more some $55 billion in tax benefits and *cut* those with less than $10,000 a year by $17 billion through raising taxes and reducing social programs. The attack on those programs struck the *working* poor with particular severity. They were overrepresented among the roughly 500,000 families removed from the AFDC rolls and the one million who lost their food stamps between 1980 and 1984. During the first Reagan administration, the poverty rate went over 15 percent for the first time in twenty years.

All of this was rationalized in supply-side theory by the assertion that it would lead to higher investment and productivity and, ultimately, to more jobs that would benefit the poor. It was, in short, "trickle down" on a truly grand scale. Only it did not work that way. The Economic Recovery Tax Act of 1981 went into effect during 1982, that is, during the worst recession in half a century. Needless to say, the rich did not put the billions they received from the tax cut into a sock. They "invested" it—and here the ambiguity of that word becomes very important—but *not* in new plant or other wealth-producing assets. This was a time of double-digit interest rates because of the monetarism of the Federal Reserve. There was cash to burn—to "invest"—for inflation hedges, speculative gains, and other such activities, but in 1982, there was a 4.7 percent *decline* in business fixed investment. When the recovery began in 1983, it did so because of old-fashioned, quite Keynesian demand-side factors.

As Edward Denison summarized the evidence, "If there is one lesson that should have been learned by now, it is that proposals that the federal government promote growth by special tax provisions or subsidies should be viewed with the greatest suspicion. The real purpose of such proposals almost invariably is to enlarge someone's income at someone else's expense. The claim that these tax changes are good for growth is incidental and usually wrong."

The supply-siders had a variety of defenses against the embarrassing data about investment. Almost all of them held that there had indeed been some unfortunate "lags," but that the predicted investment took place in 1984. At first glance, that seems plausible enough. Net investment was $50 billion in 1983 and $107 billion in 1984. So, Reagan's friends say, even if investment did not lead the way out of the recession, as it was supposed to do, it did finally go up as a result of the enormous subsidies Reagan showered upon the corporations and the rich. The corporate analyst Michael Evans was more persuasive: "The principal reason capital spending has rebounded so quickly is that it had collapsed so thoroughly during the previous years."

Benjamin Friedman of Harvard showed that the boom in capital spending in 1984 took less of a percentage of the GNP than similar outlays in the second half of the sixties. For that matter, Michael Evans noted that the ratio of capital spending to GNP in 1984 was slightly less than it had been in 1980—during the Carter administration. Even more significant, the surge in real consumer spending was much greater than that in capital investment, and the lion's share of the latter went for office equipment and automobiles, not for new plants. In short, the Reagan boom was not only consumer-led, but powered to a disturbing degree by consumer spending on credit, as private debt soared far above private income. In September 1985, a mere four years after the passage of Reagan's supply-side law to raise the rate of savings, that rate hit the lowest level ever.

But then one need not engage in abstruse statistical arguments about the failure of supply-side economics, because the Reagan White House itself proves the point. The heart of the supply-side strategy had included rapid depreciation for buildings, machines, and vehicles. But, the *Wall Street Journal* reported in 1985, one reason that the president had now proposed ending such allowances was that they had not worked! To be sure, a company like General Electric had earned $6 billion between 1981 and 1983, but paid no federal taxes and collected rebates. But, the *Journal* said, the White House, the Council of Economic Advisors, and the Treasury had concluded that these subsidies did not have their intended effect, which was why Reagan had proposed to end them. As Representative Willis Gradison made the point, "accelerated depreciation led to negative tax rates and uneconomic investment in many areas."

These trends are rather obviously disturbing from a point of view of equity and justice. The rich prospered, the poor became poorer. The huge deficits which, in perverse Keynesian fashion did indeed stimulate the economy and promote recovery, were the result of a structural transfer of tax burdens from the top to the middle and the bottom, of the high public costs of the recession that helped defeat inflation, and of the enormous increase in military spending.

But leave justice aside for the moment. *The way in which the Reagan recovery was achieved has created an economic time bomb that will explode at some point in the future.*

II

President Reagan thus adopted the new supply-side radicalism, but he did not simultaneously give up the old austerity. His monetarism was traditional and restrictive, even as his tax and military policies were expansive. Tight money and high interest rates did indeed end inflation, but with immediate and quite negative consequences. In this case, then, it is not necessary to predict future troubles as a result of administration actions. They have already happened.

When Reagan became president, he found that his most enthusiastic supporters were ranged along opposite sides of an ideological chasm. In his genial, charismatic way he simply embraced the contraries. His tax cuts were the Keynesian accelerator; his monetarism (which was, of course, actually carried out by the Federal Reserve) was the brake. But even though those policies worked against one another, they shared an underlying effect: They both shifted income from those most in need to the very wealthy.

In fairness, it should be recorded at the outset that it was Jimmy Carter who made the initial turn to monetarism in 1979 when he put Paul Volcker in charge of the Fed. But the Reaganites, although aggressively pursuing a contradiction, were much more forthright than Carter was. Monetarism was, for them, the Old Cause, not a reluctant heresy. "Inflation," the Council of Economic Advisors said in the first report published under the new administration, "is a monetary phenomenon." The OPEC price increase, it was acknowledged, had had some effect, but the basic problem of the economy was to be found in the liberal addiction to cheap money. If, the monetarists patiently explained, the money supply did not rise in tandem with prices, then the latter had to give.

There would be, the Council admitted, "a short-lived trade off between unemployment and the rate of inflation. This means that policies designed to reduce inflation significantly will temporarily increase unemployment and reduce output growth." There are two things to be noted about this statement: It is in direct opposition to the supply-side assumptions stated elsewhere in the same report; and it turned out to be disastrously wrong. The mild transition needed to correct the "imbalances" in the economy became the worst recession of the postwar era. Then, when the Federal Reserve switched its line in late 1982 as it rescued Mexico from default on its debt—the United States lent the Mexicans the money that they paid back to the American banks, which increased the money supply in this country—monetarists, such as Milton Friedman, predicted an imminent inflationary surge. And that was wrong, too.

But in 1981 and for most of 1982, monetarism ruled and made a signal contribution to deepening the recession. In the United States, the most important immediate victims were to be found in the auto and construction industries, both of them highly sensitive to interest rates that tight money had pushed up sky-high. Massive layoffs resulted. This savage attack on working people was a key to the Reagan recovery *and* a source of structural unemployment. Its immediate result was, however, unmistakable. Pricing millions of Americans out of those cars and houses, and the other interest-sensitive purchases, it was a prime cause of the double-digit joblessness of 1982 and early 1983.

There was also a Catch 22. When the ravages of the maxi-recession did finally bring down the inflation rate, it did so by exceedingly high interest rates, which led to the overvaluation of the dollar. That made foreign imports cheaper and American exports more expensive, and therefore had the effect of reducing employment in manufacturing (which is exported) while almost all of the new jobs were opened up in the services (which is, thus far, primarily domestic). This was one of the many reasons employment did not rise in that sector, even though there was exceedingly high growth. Moreover, those old antagonists, monetarism and supply-side economics, did work together—but in a perverse way. For the interest rates stayed high even though inflation was low because the financial markets were understandably worried about the gargantuan deficits that Reagan had created.

There was a special irony in the case of one of the victims of this process: the capital-goods industry. According to the supply-side gospel, one would have thought it would have been a prime beneficiary of an investment boom. But when that belated, and quite moderate, surge did finally come on the heels of a consumer boom, monetary policy helped to price American capital goods out of the market *in the United States itself*. The South Koreans and the West Germans led in taking half of that market away from the American companies. And that was something more than an episode, since this industry is a critical determinant of future economic performance, operating as it does on the frontiers of technology.

These trends had a particularly cruel impact upon the Third World. The poor countries, and even the "new middle class of nations" in Latin America, such as Mexico, Argentina, and Brazil, became very dependent on Western, and particularly American, banks in the 1970s. But when the interest rates soared even as the United States and the world went into recession, the interest charges on the enormous Third World debt went up while their ability to pay declined. By 1985, that debt, mainly concentrated in a few countries, had reached $900 billion, and interest payments absorbed about 25 percent of the export earnings of the nonoil economies in the South.

To make matters worse, there was a significant drop in the prices the Third World received for its food and raw materials. This constituted what the London *Economist* called "the poor man's gift" to the rich and it was worth $65 billion in 1984–85. Indeed, by mid-1985, even Reagan's secretary of the treasury made some halfhearted moves to get relief. Characteristically they focused on governmental guarantees for private banks to allow them to lend even more to the Third World.

The Europeans were hurt by monetarism, too. The most dramatic casualty was the French Socialist government, which saw the flight of capital facilitated by the high interest rates in the United States during 1981 and 1982. Why should business, which was largely hostile to Mitterrand in any case, risk money creating jobs in France when they could get such a high return from Treasury bills in the United States? This meant, as prominent German Socialist economist Fritz Scharp remarked in 1985, that a national Keynesian fiscal policy is now impossible if interest rates rise on the world market.

At first glance, it would seem that there was, however, a clear winner in all of this financial turmoil: Ronald Reagan's America. And, in the short run, the influx of foreign funds helped exempt Reagan, the ranking capitalist ideologue in the world, from the rules of capitalism. If Washington had been forced to pay for those enormous deficits with American borrowing alone, then the specter of "crowding out," falsely raised by William Simon in the mid-seventies, would have finally come true. That is, government borrowing—by a fiscally irresponsible conservative administration supported by the same William Simon—would have been so high that it would have bid up the price of money to such levels that the private sector would have had difficulty raising its funds in the market.

Foreign investors protected Reagan from that fate. When it was announced in 1985 that the United States had become a debtor nation for the first time since before World War I, the lives of most Americans were not affected. It was just another one of those curious facts that the experts and their computers generate in their compulsive way. And Mr. Reagan assured his countrymen that it made little difference in the real world. He was right as long as the American economy continued to grow and foreign creditors were satisfied. But the moment that there was a downturn, or some other economic-political disturbance in the status quo, the United States was vulnerable to pressures from abroad to an unprecedented degree. For this economy has become a sort of Ponzi game in which old debt is repaid with new debt, and it now takes but a single interruption of that process to set off a chain reaction. We are dependent upon the "confidence" of foreign investors as never before in this century.

At the same time, monetarism increased inequality within the United States. Net interest as a percentage of the federal budget rose sharply as the deficit increased and had to be financed at very high interest rates. In the Reagan projections for 1986, net interest was computed at $142.5 billion—and all of the income security programs, other than social security itself, were estimated at $115.8 billion. Most of that government debt is, of course, held by wealthy individuals and institutions, and that means that paying these charges turns the tax system into a mechanism for collecting money from the middle class and working people and transferring a good part of it to the rich.

So the soaring interest rates that slew the inflationary dragon did not simply have an immediate and destructive impact upon the American workers who lost their jobs during the recession and the recovery. It worked negatively upon both Europe and the Third World, and it subverted the economic sovereignty of the United States and helped promote inequality within America.

For this analysis, however, the most significant single effect of monetarism—and of all Reagan's policies—was to reduce the social wage and thereby to begin to "unwind" the Fordist film of some fifty years' duration.

III

After all that has been said about the incoherent and contradictory nature of Reagan's policies, it would be silly to argue that there was some kind of White House "plan" to reduce the living standard of the poor and the real wages of the working people in order to make corporations more profitable. That is indeed what happened, but the administration was, in its own terms at least, lucky rather than conspiratorial.

So the results were the accidental outcome of a sincerely held, intentional social meanness, of a conservative bias against the lowest orders, which linked together the most heterogeneous initiatives, rather than of a theory. Even if Keynesianism for the rich and monetarism were implacable enemies of one another, they shared the basic value that the working people and the poor were simply getting too much money and that the solution was to cut down their consumption.

That is how I would explain the reactionary rationale that one seems to find in the Reagan assault on organized and unorganized labor. Like his hero, Franklin Roosevelt, but with fundamentally different values, Reagan acted on political instincts. His underlying logic was well put by Gottfried Habler of Harvard in an American Enterprise Institute study: "In recent years, more and more economists have reached the conclusion that a full and sustained recovery from the present recession will require a moderate reduction in real wages, in all industrial countries (with the possible exception of Japan), to bring about a shift in income distribution from wages and salaries to profits for the purpose of stimulating investment and growth."

That is precisely what Mr. Reagan did whether he was aware of the meanings of his actions or not.

In retrospect, the smashing of the Professional Air Traffic Controllers' (PATCO) strike in 1981 might be interpreted as the opening signal in an antilabor offensive. Labor, as we have seen, had lost a part of its power base in a society that was shifting from manufacturing to service employment and from the Northeast and Midwest to the antilabor South and Southwest. And the unions had suffered political defeats during the Carter administration even when the White House and the Congress were both in Democratic hands for the first time in a decade. Labor-law reform, a top priority of the AFL-CIO, was ignominiously defeated.

When Reagan turned on PATCO, a confident and growing union movement might have been able to respond dramatically. But the flight controllers were unpopular because they had supported Reagan's candidacy in 1980, ironically in order to gain a bargaining edge in the 1981 negotiations. And, in any case, a union that went out in sympathy with a strike that was illegal under federal law—even though quite justified—opened itself up to crippling legal and financial damage. Had labor been in a more militant stance generally, it might have disregarded the technicalities and counted on economic power to force a settlement of the PATCO dispute. But the unions were on the defensive and had little public support in a nation that had just elected Ronald Reagan.

Whatever the reason, the AFL-CIO and its affiliates did not challenge Reagan forcefully on the PATCO issue. And at almost the same time that the president was carrying out the largest mass firings in labor history, the economy went into a deep recession. Historically, mass layoffs have been the most efficient single antidote to worker militancy. With "prime" workers—white males between twenty-five and thirty-five years of age—suffering jobless rates previously reserved for minorities, management was in a good bargaining position with even the strongest unions. The Auto Workers, once the trendsetters in making new gains, now made concessions to the Big Three as many of their advances of the past were taken back by the companies.

In other cases, corporations used the crisis to negotiate Employee Stock Ownership Plans (ESOPs) that gave a semblance, but sometimes not even that, of worker control in return for very real federal subsidies. In some instances, desperate workers bought out failing enterprises in an attempt to keep their own jobs by "voluntarily" downgrading their wages. At the same time, there was an increase in "two-tier" labor agreements in which new hires received lower wages than the labor force already in place. In 1983, 5 percent of collective-bargaining agreements had a two-tier feature; in 1984, 8 percent (the percentages in the service sector were higher: 9 percent in 1983 and 17 percent in 1984).

Meanwhile, the giant multinationals were able to farm out more and more of their work to the Third World where wage and other costs were much cheaper. And even when the Japanese opened up auto plants in the United States, they regularly imported the higher technology components from home. But by then all the big American auto companies had made a joint arrangement with their "competitors" in Japan and were well on the way to creating an international automobile whose parts could be built in factories situated in other parts of the globe, even if the final product was assembled in this country.

There was also a general increase in part-time work throughout the entire economy. Such employment provides no fringe benefits and is almost impossible to organize on any large scale. This trend was most marked in trade (with one-third of the employees part-time) and services (two-fifths). Labor was being hit by the cyclical impact of high unemployment and by structural trends such as multinationalization and part-time work. By February of 1985, the situation had become so threatening that an AFL-CIO committee proposed a radical rethinking of traditional methods of organizing, including the concept of an "associate membership" in unions. It ruefully noted that former members of unions were now much more numerous in the United States than present members.

The cumulative impact of all this upon wages was that, as the Federal Reserve Bulletin reported in December 1984, since 1979 one out of six trade unions had had to accept contracts that "freeze or reduce wages and fringe benefits or alter work rules." The Bulletin continued, "by 1982, wage freezes and pay cuts had become as commonplace as wage increases in collective-bargaining settlements. Moreover, despite the rebound in economic activity and in profits since late 1982, managements have continued to press for cost-reduction measures, and wage cuts and freezes remained prominent features of union negotiations in 1984."

To be fair, real wages had started to fall before Ronald Reagan became president—and at a much faster rate in the United States than in Europe. There was a 3.4 percent increase in hourly rates between 1962 and 1969, a fall of .3 of one percent between 1973 and 1975, and a modest increase of 1.9 percent between 1975 and 1978. Reagan's policies now gave these tendencies a massive, governmental push in the wrong direction. In 1981 and 1982, real hourly earnings fell to levels that had already been achieved in the late sixties and were around 8 percent less than they had been in 1972.

We have already noted one of the reasons this drop in real wages was less of an economic disaster than it might have been: the increase in two-income families as women flooded into the labor market. There were analysts at the Brookings Institution who blamed those same women for structurally inflating the unemployment rate; if they had stayed in the kitchen there would have been more work for men. But if that reactionary dream had actually taken place, it would have helped to create an even more severe recession, and perhaps a depression, in 1982–83.

Another reason for the limited damage of the worst downturn in half a century was credit. As income fell, debt rose. Indeed, it was during the recovery years of 1982–1985 that there was a marked escalation in consumer loans that could not be collected. There were less than $1 billion of them at the end of 1983, close to $2.5 billion in late 1985. However, that did not deter the banks, which had promoted the international financial crisis by their frenzied policies in the seventies, from handing out credit cards in a similarly reckless fashion in the eighties.

Cards, the *Wall Street Journal* reported in December 1985, have been sent to prisoners, unemployed teenagers, and even a few household pets. A San Diego secretary, with an income of $16,100 a year, received, unasked, three cards with a total line of credit of $15,000. She declared bankruptcy in less than a year. "After three years of wild growth," the *Journal* commented, "consumer debt is fast becoming another sinkhole in lenders' credit swamp. Beyond the jolt that threatens an already shaky banking industry, a growing number of economists cite such evidence as October's record monthly drop in retail sales as signals that a deterioration in consumer debt has spilled over in the general economy, menacing the recovery and possibly presaging another recession."

But if the Reagan administration drove down the real wages of the working people and forced families to take on debt burdens that were dangerously high for them as well as the economy, why did Reagan win reelection by a landslide in 1984?

The answer to that question is obviously complex, but one aspect of it is particularly relevant here. Political scientists have rather rigorously worked out the correlation between economic events and their political impact. Eight quarters (two years) after any significant change (sharp inflation, declining real income, unemployment, etc.), political attitudes have discounted the event. As a Brookings essay made this point, "This means that performance during the first half of an administration need not affect its support in the second half. Thus the Reagan administration suffered no lasting harm from presiding over the deepest recession since the 1930s during its first two years."

In the fall of 1982, only slightly more than 40 percent of the American people approved of the way Reagan carried out his job. Had the presidential election been held at that time, it might have been quite a different story than in 1984. When the actual election did come, there were those who had been furious with Reagan in 1982 because his policies had forced their layoff and who now voted for the president in 1984 because the recovery had put them back to work.

The political effect of a drastic reduction in real income dissipates within two years. The economic effects do not. In the perspective of this book, Ronald Reagan had blundered into the recovery because he showed business that it could make money once again. But that happened, in some measure, because labor costs were reduced by the attack on unions and the "upscale" market for the upper middle class and the rich expanded as a result of Reagan's income redistribution. It was a consequence of a pre-Keynesian attack on labor and a perverse Keynesian stimulation of the economy via the rich and the military.

All of this is fine for a while, and it has made Mr. Reagan look very much like a winner for a while. And yet, as we have seen, the economy is booby-trapped: The lowered consumption of the mass of people holds out the possibility of a crisis of underconsumption and the return of the problems of the twenties; the wild growth of corporate and consumer credit, and the speculation that is rampant throughout the society, could all trigger crises; and so on.

Most of these negative trends were, as noted, already in motion before Ronald Reagan came to office. He simply made the worst of a bad situation. Between 1968 and 1984, as Lester Thurow computes the data, the percentage of middle-income households (those with incomes of between 75 percent and 125 percent of the median) had fallen from 27.1 percent to 23.2 percent of total households. At the same time, the number of low-income households had risen from 36.1 percent to 39.4 percent of the total. Now that is obviously a misery for those who suffer downward social mobility. But in addition to those individual tragedies, this development means that the middle class–oriented income structure that had been the great innovation of Fordism and a key to the prosperity of the entire society has been subverted. Serious trouble for everyone cannot be too far behind.

The monetarist conservatives of the last generation, as I have remarked, outlined a sort of Greek tragedy, only in economic terms. The hubris of the New Deal liberals and the European Socialists created the conditions that were to bring them to a terrible fate. When half a century intervenes between cause and effect, such a scenario is not too convincing. Of course, as I have insisted throughout this book, the consequences of Fordist success, and then of Reagan's recovery, contained seeds of future disasters but they cannot be reduced to a single monetarist cause even though that factor is at work.

I suspect we will not have to wait half a century for Mr. Reagan's fate. That is why I argue that there will be at least an opening for the next Left within the next five or so years. And when it comes, for all the difficulties that a confused and even bankrupt Left now faces, it will turn out that Mr. Reagan's revolution wasn't very revolutionary after all.

IV

Franklin Roosevelt created new institutions: social security, above all; the National Labor Relations Board; programs for health, education, and welfare, which acquired their own very loyal constituencies; and through Roosevelt's heirs, Medicare and Medicaid. These were formal transformations that changed the very nature of life in this country. When the Republicans finally conquered the presidency in 1952, they actually legitimated, by accepting, the reforms they had been denouncing since the thirties.

Even Ronald Reagan has been at pains for years to deny that he ever said that he wanted to make social security voluntary. That institution may be changed in this or that detail but it has become a fixture of American life, much as national health in Britain is supported by Tories as well as Socialists.

What was the great institutional shift of the first Reagan administration? A tax act. There were, of course, many other reactionary policies, but none of them took the form of a new and irreversible institution. And, if the next Left can work within the framework of some kind of overall perspective, it does not need a constitutional amendment, but simply a majority in the Congress and a Democratic president, to reverse the priorities of that tax act.

Coming to terms with the Reagan past, if and when it explodes, will not be too difficult. Creating an alternative future is a more serious question.

6

The End of the Left?

Does the abject failure of the Socialist government in France signal the end of the Western Left?

At first glance, the evidence for that proposition seems obvious. President Mitterrand and the French Socialists received an absolute majority in 1981 and proceeded faithfully to carry out a program that had been carefully worked out over a decade. Within a year they were forced to sound retreat and by the spring of 1983 they had effectively reversed almost every priority of their original plan. If their economic performance improved after 1983, their critics said (including not a few on the left) it was largely because they acted on classic conservative principles. Indeed, shortly after this *volte-face*, Jacques Delors, the Socialist minister most responsible for the change, baited the Right: "The Socialists are in the process of making the adjustment that the Barre government [the conservative administration they had attacked and defeated in 1981] did not dare to do, politically or in terms of the social classes."

Had a movement that had boldly promised a "rupture with capitalism" on the road to power become more capitalist than the capitalists once in power? If the answer is yes, isn't that an obituary for the dreams of the entire Western Left?

The American Left might plead in mitigation that Mitterrand is a socialist and that his defeat therefore does not imply the failure of American liberalism. But the French Socialist program was a principled Keynesianism—much more decent in its social values than any variant of that philosophy ever practiced in this country—but Keynesianism nevertheless. So can't it be fairly said that the French failure was a defeat for the orthodoxy of the entire Western Left during the past half a century?

Of course. There is no doubt that the Fordist strategy is now bankrupt and that the first year of Mitterrand's rule was a painful demonstration of that fact. Yet it is wrong to equate that specific expression of the Left vision with the vision itself. It is by no means guaranteed that the Left will come up with a new and viable application of its principles, but it is by no means excluded either.

Before we can turn to that possible future it is necessary to learn all of the bitter lessons of the immediate French past. The unmistakable failures and half successes of that experience can teach a very positive lesson.

One of the reasons I insist on this point is quite "American." During the period of the Reagan recovery, there was an illusion in the United States, very much shared by the leaders of the opposition and a large part of the public in France, that the contrast between Reagan's triumph and Mitterrand's frustration defined the line between the obsolete past in Paris and the relevant future in Washington. America, it was widely believed, had found a new mode of economic growth and progress at the very time that the French Left had so dramatically demonstrated its inability to cope with an unprecedented reality. But what happened in France was far more complex than most Americans, and many French, think.

Mitterrand was defeated because France could not afford to run a relatively large internal (governmental) deficit and an external (balance-of-trade) deficit at the same time. But in both of these areas, Ronald Reagan's deficits were, as a percentage of the GNP, much larger than Mitterrand's. By one of those miserable ironies in which history seems to take delight, the capitalist ideologue was exempt from the very rules that he so sternly preached, but those constraints operated with great rigor against the Socialist who wanted to violate them.

Let me put the point paradoxically: *The only country in which the French Socialist program might have worked—because it could ignore those internal and external constraints, for a time at least—was the United States of America!* The Bank for International Settlements, a key institution of the world capitalist system in the years of crisis, understood this point very well. "The current U.S. expansion," it said in 1985, "is simply not exportable: No government outside the United States could safely base a stimulative fiscal policy on the assumption that it will extract spontaneous external financing on a durable basis."

But then, as the last chapter suggested, the "American option" is not open to the United States in the long run either. Adam Smith will eventually take revenge on his faithless disciple, Ronald Reagan. The White House did not blaze a path to a new age, but stumbled into a politically comfortable parenthesis between two ages.

I do not say these things in order to belittle the significance of the French Socialist reversal. The Left must examine that event in the most careful and candid way, for it bears upon how the future is to be created. More subtly, Alain Minc suggested that there is something of a mystery about why Léon Blum's Popular Front program failed in the mid-thirties and then worked after World War II. In Mitterrand's case, too, history will look back and discover that some innovations that were overwhelmed by a tidal wave of economic change were shrewd and usable reforms. I want to be instructed by the positive accomplishments of the French Socialists as well as by their mistakes. For both are relevant to the creation of my possible future.

I

When François Mitterrand came to power in 1981, he promised a "rupture with capitalism." If his policies of the first year were not the clean break with the past they were supposed to be, they were an audaciously consistent and quite socialist version of that Keynesianism that, in its technocratic guise, had dominated France since 1945. One might argue that Mitterrand had discovered, and followed the path of, that radical John Maynard Keynes defined by Joan Robinson and systematically ignored in Britain and the United States. The French Center-Right, which dominated the postwar period until Mitterrand's victory, imitated the more conventional Keynes. As Jacques Chirac, one of the leaders of the anti-Socialist opposition, put it in 1985, "the social democratic model of society . . . more or less inspired all of the governments of our country since the Liberation."

France, then, was a case in point of the triumph of Fordism throughout the West. There was an ironic confirmation of this fact, largely unrecognized at the time, which was to cause Mitterrand trouble after he took power. In the months prior to the election, the arch free marketeer of France and prime minister under Giscard, Raymond Barre, took some planks from the Socialist program that he was denouncing and attempted to use government power to reflate the economy in time for the vote. He provided various subsidies and cut the payroll contributions for medical care. But, since the cost of health care continued to rise, this stimulus helped create the "Mitterrand" deficit of 1982. The point, however, is not to excuse Mitterrand by indicting Barre, but to say that Fordist assumptions were shared—Left, Right, and Center—in France in 1981.

And yet, Mitterrand's version of Fordism was distinctively socialist in both the traditional and new sense of the word. On the one hand, the benefits he inaugurated were systematically biased toward the poorest people in the society; on the other hand he sought to create not simply growth, but a new model of consumption, a qualitative rather than a quantitative change. He simultaneously insisted on an industrial policy that was to be based on a dynamic nationalized sector, and pushed for the reduction of the workweek and year. He honored the clenched fist of working-class history and the poetic rose of May 1968.

Strangely enough, one critical problem with the application of this vision had to do with the Socialists' failure to understand how badly their predecessors had managed the economy. If they realized that Giscard and Barre had structurally weakened France so that the old Gaullist *dirigisme* no longer worked, they might have hesitated in trying to create a much more imaginative, "'68-ish," version of that same system. Perhaps a bit of history is in order to place this into its proper context.

French capitalism before World War II had been paternalistic, family-controlled, anti-innovative. Unions were weak—their strength rose sharply during the Popular Front but declined quickly after the brief interlude—and national labor legislation, like mandatory vacations, was much more important than collective-bargaining agreements. The Resistance was conscious of these trends and was determined not simply to defeat the Nazis, but to build a new society after the victory. Communists, Socialists, and social Catholics, as well as General de Gaulle himself, were committed to a new beginning. As Richard Kuisel put it, "What was unique about France was the way a collective sense of national decline and disenchantment with the liberal [free-enterprise] order provided the fundamental impetus for change."

There were those who even expected "the tomorrows that sing." They did not, of course, come, but there was a considerable transformation in that first period after the Liberation. Consumption was partially socialized as it was in every Western nation. But there was a distinctively French accent to this Fordism. The social security system, which was set up in 1945, was supposed to provide a "general regime" for everyone in the country, but Gallic corporatism soon amended that dream. The system was modified by "special regimes" that favored the interests of particular groups, and it was financed in a way that helped the middle and upper classes and discriminated against the workers. There was also a considerable nationalization of industry, including the takeover of Renault, destined to be a symbol of left-wing success for years to come.

This was the period when Jean Monnet and his associates introduced the idea and practice of national planning (which they borrowed in part from the American experience with the War Production Board, a success the United States was determined to forget as quickly as possible). As time went on, structural changes that had been undertaken in the name of a radical future became increasingly technocratic. French "indicative planning" has been rightly called a "conspiracy in the public interest" on the part of the corporations and the government—a conspiracy that, not surprisingly, enormously benefited the corporate conspirators.

When de Gaulle returned to power in 1958, and particularly after the Algerian war ended in the early sixties, there was another period of rapid economic and social transformation. De Gaulle embraced a supply-side Fordism with a vengeance as the state was mobilized to create large-scale industries capable of competing on the world market. Between 1960 and 1973—the heyday of the Great Prosperity—the GDP rose by 5.6 percent (almost double the rate of the seventies). The blue-collar working class, one of the surest signs of Fordist development, rose by 50 percent, compared to a 33 percent increase in the labor force as a whole. But at the same time, there was a considerable growth in the new salaried strata, a harbinger of the coming crisis of Fordism *and* an important constituency for a revived French Socialism.

During those Gaullist years of modernization and national Keynesianism, real wages were held down in order to finance the rationalization of the economy. More broadly, there was social traditionalism even as economic change was radically transforming the country. So it was that, in 1968, a student revolt against the bureaucratic conservatism of the educational system set off a general strike of the working class. That explosion was part of a similar phenomenon that occurred throughout the West as the very success of Fordism emboldened both the workers and the emergent social strata. The barricades of revolutionary students in the Latin Quarter got most of the world media attention in France in 1968, but that was only the most obvious aspect of a complex event.

The economic agreements between the government and the workers (the "rue de Grenelle" compact) had a much more profound impact on France than the graffiti on the Sorbonne walls, symptomatic as the latter were. The minimum wage was indexed and raised by 30 percent; the average wage was increased by 11 percent. This was part of a larger trend whereby the social wage in France went up dramatically throughout the late sixties and seventies. De Gaulle and the conservatives thus responded to the first signs of a crisis by an intensification of the Fordist strategy.

It was, however, Valéry Giscard d'Estaing who was to face up to the crisis itself in the seventies. He became president just as the French, and world, economies entered the recession of 1974–75. But he did not turn his back on the social-wage policies that de Gaulle had adopted in 1968. On the contrary, Giscard presented himself as a "social democrat" of sorts, paying a visit to a prison where he shook hands with some of the inmates, inviting a group of immigrant workers to breakfast with him at the Élysée Palace.

Then, in 1975, Giscard's prime minister, Jacques Chirac, launched a government-stimulated recovery with large export subsidies. Like Mitterrand later, Giscard faced both a balance-of-payments and an inflation problem shortly after he undertook his expansionist program. In part, these "leftist" responses to the crisis—including measures that made it more difficult to fire a worker—were a tribute to the fact that Mitterrand had come within 1 percent of winning the presidency in 1974 and that the Union of the Left, which united the Socialists and the Communists, seemed to have the potential of gaining a majority in the National Assembly in 1978.

But then in 1976 Giscard appointed Raymond Barre prime minister and finally made a turn to the right, a move that was facilitated by the breakdown of the Union of the Left when the Communists realized that they had become junior partners in the alliance. Even with Giscard's shift, though, the conservatism was primarily in economic policy and the government remained committed to high social expenditures despite lowered growth rates. Between 1965 and 1973, the public spending portion of the GDP was around 35–36 percent. By 1978, it had climbed to 39.5 percent and in 1980, it reached 42.8 percent. Transfer payments had accounted for 20.1 percent of disposable income in 1970; they had reached 33.7 percent by 1980. All this, mind you, under the

"Right," which has now developed the usual case of amnesia about its own history.

But Giscard did change on the economic front, a fact that was to have fateful consequences for Mitterrand and the Socialists. While de Gaulle had sought to create a coherent and modern economy within France, Giscard and Barre followed a line of "industrial redeployment." The government would no longer support the "crippled ducks" of industry. Rather, it would adapt France to the world market, emphasizing those productive activities that it could do best (the "*créneaux*") and relying on imports for the rest.

Exports did indeed climb—but weighted in the direction of the Third World—and so did imports. The latter were high-tech capital and consumer goods, and their importance was underlined by an increasing foreign presence within the French economy itself. At the beginning of the Common Market, France produced 85 percent of its equipment needs, but when the crisis hit in the seventies, that figure had dropped to 74 percent. The dependence on capital goods was even more severe, reaching 50 percent under Giscard. That meant that rapid expansion tended to yield an increasing balance-of-payments deficit as foreign machines were installed in French factories. Growth had become, in part at least, perverse, as de Gaulle's heirs mortgaged French economic sovereignty and made the general's worst dreams come true—but under circumstances that were to bedevil his most severe critics.

Ironically, the Socialist critique of Giscard in the 1981 electoral campaign was too gentle. They did not realize how profoundly he had undercut that Gaullist idea of a self-sufficient France, or how rundown the industrial plant had been allowed to become. Worse, they made the same underestimation of conservative failure when they prepared their own plans.

The London *Economist* summarized the consequences in a 1984 retrospect on Mitterrand's victory: "The Socialists thought they would nationalize a phalanx of rich industrial concerns that could be used to boost output, jobs, and national wealth. Instead, with one or two exceptions, the state had acquired, at high cost, a collection of debt-ridden, wheezing remnants of the go-go years of Gaullist giantism." The moderate Fordism of the Right had failed—and now the Socialists proposed to initiate a radical Fordism on that structurally flawed base.

If it is fair to argue that François Mitterrand inherited many pressing problems from his conservative predecessors, one must add, as Alain Lipietz has remarked, that it was inexcusable for the Socialists to have been ignorant of that fact. They summoned the nation to take a voyage of economic adventure in a leaky boat. That conservatives were responsible for most of the leaks must be taken into consideration in any moral accounting—but it is politically and economically irrelevant.

II

Strangely, the French Socialist experience was dramatic proof of an eminently left-wing theory. Mitterrand and company had insisted strenuously on this point while on the road to power—and then ignored it in the moment of their triumph.

Capitalism, they rightly said, had a powerful logic of its own. It demanded, for instance, a certain minimal level of profits to make the system work, since even a nationalized enterprise must have a surplus to finance new investment and depreciation. In a mixed economy, there was a rationale for the socialist promotion of profits in both the public and private sectors. The Social Democrats of Europe, the French Left went on to say, had obeyed this capitalist imperative and therefore, even though they had made significant reforms, they had done little or nothing to change the structure of power and wealth.

We are not "social democrats," the French insisted prior to 1981; we are "socialists." The "rupture with capitalism" was supposed to create a radical-system logic based upon the creation of a new, decentralized mode of social life and of worker participation in all management decisions. In fact, the French Socialists in power were driven to adapt themselves to capitalism to a much greater degree than the Social Democrats who had the good for-

tune to come in during the Great Prosperity, when there was
some room to maneuver, and not during the crisis.

Let me be fair. Mitterrand and his comrades had collided with
the structural problem described in chapter 2, and it is neither
French nor confined to the eighties. How does the Left gradually
and democratically transform a system when it must operate
within that system? If one abandons the Leninist illusion that it
is possible in an advanced capitalist democracy simply to "smash"
the bourgeois state and proceed to the revolutionary reconstruction of the entire society—as most European Communists
and all European Socialists had done by 1981—then how does one
carry out radical change within these constraints?

That problem has been around since the end of World War I
when the Socialist parties of Europe were suddenly confronted
with the contradictions of partial, limited power within a system
hostile to that power. The agitator's myth of a sudden, dramatic
leap from capitalism to socialism perished the minute such a reality intervened. In 1981, in France—that is, in the middle of a
world crisis in a second-rank economy—these limitations were
intolerable. Yet the Socialists, at the moment of Fordist failure,
looked for the kind of economic growth only attained at the
height of Fordist success.

One reason for this error was that the French Left had been
in opposition too long. Between 1928 and 1958, the parties of the
Left—the Socialists, Communists, and Radicals—had won a majority in every election, but had been unable to unite, and leadership passed to the Center Right. Then, from 1958 to 1981, de
Gaulle and his heirs utterly dominated the Fifth Republic. During more than half a century, then, one counted the periods of
Left dominance in months. Indeed, there was even a mystique
that made a virtue out of this tragedy: It was seen as a glory of
the Popular Front that it put through its reforms quickly and
then failed. Now, however, Mitterrand's seven-year presidency
and the Socialists' absolute majority in the Assembly did not allow the luxury of such glorious defeats. They were stuck with
power. What were they going to do with it?

When François Mitterrand first managed to recreate a Socialist party in 1971, the Left was still under the spell of the dramatic events of May 1968. So the first program was both "Marxistical" (*marxisant* in French) and 1968-ish. It talked of both "the dictatorship of profit" and of a "new model of growth." It was not enough, the Socialists said, simply to live better. One must live in a new way. But when the rhetoric was discounted, the policy prescriptions were Keynesian—radically Keynesian, but Keynesian nevertheless.

Mass consumption, the 1971 program argued in the classic Fordist mode, is necessary for capital accumulation. So "the struggle for the increase in wages is far from counterposed in itself to the logic of the capitalist system." But a new accent was heard in a dispute between the Socialists and their Communist partners. The French Communists, one of the most Stalinist of parties in the democratic world, were for straightforward nationalization. But the Socialists, acting on the basis of a variety of traditions, were hostile to that idea.

Many of the tendencies in the French workers' movement in the late nineteenth and early twentieth centuries were opposed to government ownership. Proudhon, Jaurès, and Guesde were all concerned lest the "cop state" (*l'état-gendarme*) turn into the "boss state" (*l'état-patron*). Then the semianarchist focus of the '68 rising revived that suspicion and the emergent Catholic Left—sometimes called the "second Left"—took it up. The Communists stuck to their beloved Soviet model. The Socialists stressed decentralization, worker self-management, a new kind of participatory democracy at the point of production.

In 1971, the newly united Socialist party was still relatively cautious in policy matters, even though its language was bold. But then, in 1975, at the Congress of Pau, and even more dramatically in 1979, at the Congress of Metz, it announced the "rupture with capitalism." Small wonder that, on the rainy May night in 1981, when the Parisian Socialists celebrated Mitterrand's victory, there were those in the crowd who chanted, "Mitterrand, du soleil!" ("Mitterrand, give us some sunshine!") That spirit, the product of a sudden and stunning victory after years in the political wilderness, did not dispose the new government to probe the weaknesses of the system they had so relentlessly criticized.

The social policies and priorities of François Mitterrand and
Ronald Reagan were diametrically opposed. Yet the socialist
strategy of the one and the supply-side tactics of the other shared
a common assumption: that growth on the old Fordist model
was still quite possible (Reaganites, like the economist Arthur
Laffer, often described themselves as John Kennedy Keynesians). Reagan, we have seen, did indeed stumble into a demand-
side Keynesian recovery that had little to do with his program
and much to do with the exceptional position of the United States
in the world. But unlike Reagan, Mitterrand was not temporarily
exempt from the rules of the market. So he failed in the great
experiment of 1981–82, and then, ironically, did rather well in
following capitalist policies with socialist modifications between
1982 and 1986. This, however, is not what he and the French Socialists had in mind.

One of the centerpieces of the first Mitterrand year—during
which practically every campaign promise was redeemed—was
the increase in buying power for the least-paid workers. The
minimum-wage law in France was baptized the "*Salaire Minimum Interprofessionnel de Croissance*" ("the Minimum Wage of
Growth") after 1968 when all sides were agreed that growth
would go on forever. The inevitable acronym for the law was *le
SMIC*, and those who received that wage were called the
smicards. They were, and are, the rough equivalent of the working poor in the United States. The new government practiced a
"solidaristic" wage policy, i.e., they provided the greatest increases for those at the bottom of the occupational structure in
an attempt to decrease inequality in the working class. Between
March of 1981, shortly before the Mitterrand victory, and July of
1982, when second thoughts had already begun, the *smicards*
saw their pay rise by 29 percent. In the economy as a whole, the
average hourly wage went up by 16 percent between the first trimester of 1981 and the first trimester of 1982. Given the double-
digit inflation inherited from Giscard and Barre, that translated
into an increase in real buying power of 3.5 percent. At the same
time, social benefits, measured in real terms, went up by 6.2
percent.

The French Socialists were well aware that such policies

would, all other things being equal, increase the cost of labor, particularly in small and medium enterprises (which were more likely to have low-wage workers) and in labor-intensive industries. But they assumed that the virtuous circle of growth would, on the classic Fordist model, save them from that contradiction. After all, the experts at the Organization for Economic Cooperation and Development (OECD)—an exclusive club of the rich nations—predicted in June of 1981 that the world economy was on the way to recovery and said that its member countries would experience 2 percent growth in GNP volume in 1982, with a brisk increase in trade as well. If that had happened, if the French recovery of 1981–82 had been part of a worldwide surge, then all of the Socialists' problems would hardly have been solved, but they would certainly have been much easier to deal with.

So the Socialists thought—and the idea was not at all preposterous at the time—that their social expenditures would enlarge the market and encourage business to expand. Then, even though wages were going up, unit costs would come down because of a huge increase in volume and productivity gains from an optimistic work force. And in the second half of 1981, France did indeed buck the international trends, in part—ironically—because of Raymond Barre's attempt to put Keynesianism to work reelecting Giscard. *But the expansion was nowhere near vigorous enough to compensate for the rise in wage costs resulting from Mitterrand's eminently decent policies.*

A maverick French economist who sometimes advised Mitterrand in this period, Serge-Christophe Kolm, drew some important conclusions from this experience. It is almost always wrong, Kolm argued, to try to redistribute income through wage increases because there is always the danger that such a policy will work, as it did in France in 1981–82, as an employment disincentive. One should finance transfers from the better-off to the worst-off, he continued, by means that do not have a negative impact on the cost of production (either through income taxes or through profit-sharing not proportionate to wages, i.e., benefiting the lowest-paid the most, etc.).

Wage policy, then, for all of its excellent social values, had the unintended consequence of making it more difficult for an enterprise to hire new workers. And yet, even though I am convinced by Kolm's practical advice, it must be added that, if the hoped-for expansion had really taken place, the negative impact would have been considerably less. It would be a major error to reject some of the French Socialists' innovations that failed, not because they were inherently wrong, but because of the impossible conditions under which they were carried out. The "contracts of solidarity" are an excellent case in point.

With great imagination, the government offered a subsidy—significantly, a reduction in social security payments for new hires—to businesses that would "contract" to reduce the work day by more than two hours. In the first and strictest formulation of the policy, the company only got the tax cut if it actually employed new workers. Later on, it was realized that it was quite possible such reductions in working hours might reduce the number of firings, which was the social equivalent of new hires, and the rules were relaxed. Still, it must be sadly noted that the contracts of solidarity did not even begin to create the employment the Socialists hoped for. But the reason was that even those corporations that participated, *under the economic conditions in France at that time*, did not take on new workers, but simply made do with fewer hands.

But if, under the full-employment policies outlined in the next chapter, it were once again possible for the Left to unite social justice and efficiency, then this way of providing very specific rewards to enterprises that accomplish a public purpose strikes me as imaginative and quite usable. There were other attempts to create jobs—more hiring in the public sector, provisions allowing early retirement at sixty, and the like—but they were overwhelmed by the contradictions of the program and the fact of the worst recession in half a century. Perhaps the most important single disappointment had to do with the failure to move toward the thirty-five-hour week. The Socialists easily introduced the fifth week of vacation for all workers as a down payment on their efforts to create employment by reducing hours *and* as a step in the direction of the new mode of life. That is clearly a permanent gain achieved by the Mitterrand government, and the opposition in power will not dare to repeal it. But when it came to the thirty-five-hour week, things became difficult and then impossible.

There is an important, and slightly misleading, chapter in French history that is relevant here. One of the major changes put through by Léon Blum in 1936 was a law that mandated two weeks of paid vacation, the forty-hour week with no reduction in pay, and put extremely rigid limits on overtime. It is the conventional historical wisdom in France, based on a misreading of the historian Alfred Sauvy, that this well-intentioned reform actually resulted in a loss in jobs.

In fact, more than 250,000 openings were created, almost 100,000 of them on the government-owned railroads where the law was most strictly enforced. It is true that these gains were short-lived, but the reason was, as Alain Fonteneau and Pierre-Alain Muet recently pointed out, that the overtime provisions created bottlenecks when industry could not find enough skilled workers. Mitterrand, it turned out, ran into problems that were even more structural than those encountered by Léon Blum.

There was a critical ambiguity in the thirty-five-hour week slogan. Did it mean thirty-five hours' work at forty hours' pay— or at thirty-five hours' pay? If the former were the case, then even the most fervent Socialist advocate of growth understood that the resulting increase in labor costs would act as a massive employment disincentive. But if it meant thirty-five hours of work for thirty-five hours of wages, then it was essentially a work-*sharing* proposal and required that employed workers be willing to take an income cut in order to open up places for their unemployed comrades. The government came out for the latter interpretation. As the minister of labor put it in February of 1982, "One simply can't have more free time and more income. It would be to deceive the French to let them think that one can have everything all at once."

The problem was, the work-sharing idea required the employed labor force to make sacrifices. Something like that happened in Sweden under Olof Palme's Socialists in 1982 and 1983. With the agreement of the unions, Palme devalued the Swedish krona, made exports more competitive, increased employment *and* reduced the real income of those with a job, most of whom had voted for him. But Sweden (and Austria, which followed similar policies) has a labor movement that organizes almost the entire work force and is committed to "solidaristic" values. French unions enrolled the smallest percentage of the labor force in Europe.

There is an important complexity here, one that Americans, with a union percentage similar to France's, don't normally understand. The more powerful a labor movement, the more pervasive its organization, the more likely it is to articulate a "general interest" rather than the particular demands of a section of the work force. In France, only the Democratic Confederation of Labor (the CFDT) supported work-sharing (it was influenced by its own Catholic heritage as well as by the Italian Communist party). The Communist-led federation as well as the more traditional business unionists all rejected sacrifice. So Mitterrand settled for thirty-nine hours' work at thirty-nine hours' pay.

The result of even this meager shift was fascinating, but not too comforting for a leftist. Productivity did rise sharply in 1982, but not because enthusiastic workers made greater effort. Rather, management tightened up its procedures and, through increased discipline, "overcompensated" for the lost time. The same thing happened, the readers of Karl Marx's *Das Kapital* will remember, when the British introduced the Ten Hours Law in the middle of the nineteenth century.

So this centerpiece of the Socialist program, a synthesis of the demands of the old and new Lefts, turned out to be quite ambivalent and resulted in the creation of very few jobs. That problem was further compounded, because the way in which the Socialist reforms were financed led to a greater deterioration in the employment situation.

The problem had already been posed—and in no way solved—under Giscard. If one tries to deal with the crisis of Fordism by raising social benefits and protecting the jobless, which Giscard did, then at a time of falling government income as a result of faltering growth it is necessary to raise taxes. In France, however, the tax system is heavily skewed toward levies on employers (in American terms, "payroll taxes"). In the eighties, income taxes took only 5.6 percent of the GDP as compared to 10.8 percent in West Germany, France's main European competitor. But total taxes—adding in social security and consumption charges—were 44.07 percent of the GDP in France as against 31.9 percent in West Germany. If, then, taxes were increased to deal with the problems of the crisis, hiring a new worker becomes more expensive, profits are reduced, investment falls, and joblessness goes up as a result.

Under such circumstances, "soaking the rich" by raising taxes on *production* is self-defeating. As Alain Lipietz well put it, "to make capital pay . . . when one expects it to create jobs is an insoluble contradiction." This is one of those utterly unfair limitations that the autocratic power of money places upon the democratic power of the electorate. There are many things that might be done about it—making the French social security tax progressive rather than regressive is an obvious step—but it is impossible, if one takes the tax system as a given, to stimulate growth through a fiscal policy that manufactures employment disincentives for business.

In Mitterrand's case, these problems were exacerbated by the hostility of bankers, national and international, to the Socialists. The "wall of money" so often evoked by the French Left is quite real, even if it is sometimes used as an excuse. In May of 1981, right after Mitterrand was elected, capital flight reached 2 billion francs a day, and the Right belligerently asserted that the Socialists would bring about a ruinous inflation. That was a case of critics living in glass houses throwing rocks. Raymond Barre's "strong franc" to curb "imported inflation" had failed miserably, and when Mitterrand took over, prices were already rising at a double-digit rate.

In the days after the presidential election, several of Mitterrand's comrades, including his arch-interparty rival, Michel Rocard, rightly told him to devalue the franc at once. But on his inauguration day, the new president told his prime minister, "One does not devalue the money of a country that has just given you a vote of confidence." Mitterrand was wrong in this proud position, but that is not to say that devaluation would have solved all his problems. It would have cheapened exports but, precisely because Giscard and Barre had so radically weakened France's industrial base, it would also have made all those capital goods that had to be imported that much more expensive. Still, on balance, devaluation would have been a positive move, and it was not made because of the euphoria attendant upon a sudden and unexpected gift of power.

There was yet another consequence of the inherited structural weaknesses of the economy: The Socialist stimulus created new jobs in West Germany, Japan, and the United States, as much as, or more than, in France. The industrial plant was simply not capable of taking advantage of the burst of prosperity that took place in the second half of 1981 and early 1982. In the first half of 1982, imports from West Germany rose by 29 percent, even though the volume of world trade was being reduced.

The "planetary New Deal" that the Socialists proposed did not save them from these contradictions. This idea owed much to Mitterrand's comrade, and president of the Socialist International, Willy Brandt. Brandt's Commission on North-South economic relations had urged an international recovery from the "common crisis" of the rich and poor lands. In this view, a concerted shift of technology and funds from North to South would create booms for the affluent as well as justice for the wretched of the earth.

That strategy was never put forward as a way out of the crisis for a single, second-rank economy. Moreover, it was hardly designed to work at a time when the nonoil Third World was still reeling from the second oil shock of 1979 and the impact of soaring American interest rates on their energy costs and debt burdens. In a sense, Giscard had made France too dependent upon its trade with the Third World. Between 1973 and 1978, when the government was vigorously subsidizing exports, commerce with the developing countries rose by a whopping 191 percent (compared to a 99 percent increase with the advanced economies). A goodly portion of those sales was classically "Fordist" goods in public projects (airports, desalination equipment, dams). Thus, the crisis of mass production struck a cruel blow at the export sector and was much more gentle with West Germany, which specialized in quality and high-tech goods.

In this setting, the vision of France taking the lead in a "planetary New Deal" was consigned to the museum of used rhetoric. The Socialists, after all, could not manage to follow their own *national* Keynesian strategy. Worse, the "external constraint," above all the limits that a growing balance-of-payments deficit placed upon Paris in its internal economic policy, became one of the principal causes of the failure of the domestic Socialist vision.

But then the Socialists had something of an answer to this constellation of problems. They were going to reshape the structure of the economy through an industrial policy based on dynamic nationalized companies. And so they did, but not at all in the way they anticipated.

III

To many people, nationalization is the sovereign leftist remedy. Mitterrand, it is thought, was acting on the basis of a worn-out formula in 1982. That is to miss the essential.

In the immediate postwar period in Europe, the nationalized sector was expanded in almost every country (the most dramatic exception was Sweden under the Socialists!). In some cases, this was done in the name of socialist (or anti-Fascist) ideals, e.g., Britain, France; in some cases, it was a result of the nationalization of enterprises that had cooperated with the Nazis, e.g., France, Austria. The experience in every case was disillusioning for a movement that once had thought public ownership was the key to justice and freedom. Nationalization bailed out incompetent private capitalists by compensating them for broken-down mines and factories; it often operated in a very capitalist fashion; and, as the crisis deepened, the public sector sometimes dug in to resist modernization and change. By 1981, there was hardly a Socialist in all of Europe who thought that nationalization was *the* innovation of the Left.

This was one of the reasons why the French Socialists talked of "self-managed" socialism, of decentralization and participatory ownership. So one of the priorities of the new Socialist government was to increase the rights of workers on the shop floor. But there was another motive for taking over from private corporations and it was somewhat strange: The Socialists were furious that the capitalists refused to behave like capitalists.

In the seventies, the nationalized sector in France had been much more dynamic than the private companies. Renault was a carmaker that was internationally competitive; the Airbus, in some ways a spin-off from the Concorde project, had taken a portion of the world airplane market away from the Americans; and in France itself, Electricity of France (EDF) and the rail system (SNCF) were fast-moving enterprises. So part of the Socialist critique of Giscard and the Right was that the capitalists had failed to carry out their traditional role of accumulation and innovation. If, they said, private enterprise would not invest in the future, then the public would have to do so.

The nationalizations, then, were somewhat schizophrenic: They were to be part of the new mode of life and, at the same time, the Archimedean point for industrial policy. The change in the human character of production was to be implemented through the Auroux laws, giving workers a voice on the factory floor; the nationalizations were to spark investment and competition. Moreover, the takeovers were focused on industries that were already semipublic (airplane construction, steel, nonferrous metals, all heavily involved with the state for years) or were considered to be vanguard technologies of national importance (electronics, chemistry, glass). There was, in short, a very empirical, nonideological argument for what Mitterrand proposed in this area.

On the day after the Socialist government decided to go ahead with the nationalizations, the newspaper *Le Quotidien de Paris* headlined a story: FRANCE ENTERED SOCIALISM YESTERDAY. That apocalyptic judgment stands in sharp contrast to the actual Socialist policy decreed for the nationalized industries some months later.

The letter to the administrators of the nationalized enterprises said: "You will seek, first of all, economic efficiency through a constant bettering of productivity. Every lack of efficiency would in effect have an impact on the entire French economy. The normal criteria of the management of industrial enterprises will apply to your group: The different activities should realize results that will assure the development of the enterprise and guarantee that the profitability of the invested capital will be normal." Alain Gomez, a founder of the Marxist left wing of the Socialist party, CERES, and a new official in the public sector, was even blunter: "My job is to get surplus value. . . . To be 'Left' is to have a certain idea of the allocation of the national wealth. This has nothing to do with the techniques that must be put in motion to produce that wealth."

What then went wrong with such an eminently practical project?

In the long run the answer is shocking: nothing. An article in the *Financial Times* noted in early 1986 that "the assets taken over in 1982 for 45 billion francs on the basis of the prevailing stock market prices . . . are now valued at about 150 billion francs. This reflects the general increase in shareprices on the Bourse which have almost trebled since the Left came to power. Additionally, the newly acquired state industrial groups have carried out successful restructuring which as private enterprises they were often unwilling or unable to do—ironically because of heavy interference from the previous right-wing administration of Mr. Valéry Giscard d'Estaing."

There is obviously a profound irony here and we will return to it when we consider whether François Mitterrand might turn out to have been the savior of French capitalism. For now, we will turn to the bad news, which was much more common than the good in the first years of Mitterrand's rule. Why did the nationalizations fail to meet their goal at that time?

One answer has already been given: the Socialists did not know how broken-down the new public properties were. Then, a policy error played an important role. At the cabinet meeting at which the decision was made to go ahead with the nationalizations, there was a fateful debate that pitted Michel Rocard, Jacques Delors, and Robert Badinter against most of the rest of the ministers and, the decisive factor, against the president. There is no need, Rocard and Delors argued, for Paris to pay for 100 percent of an enterprise that is targeted for government ownership. Fifty percent is quite enough—and much less expensive. But Mitterrand went ahead with the 100 percent buy-outs.

The consequences were, in part, not dissimilar to a corporate takeover with borrowed money in the United States. When that happened in the seventies and eighties, the acquired company had to be starved of cash in order to finance its own acquisition. Between 1981 and 1985, France paid 150 billion francs to the previous owners of newly nationalized property. It was almost impossible for a public company to show a profit while carrying such an enormous load of debt or, more precisely, for the state to do so.

Secondly, although the Auroux laws were unquestionably progressive (and, according to a survey by the London *Economist* in 1984, have even been accepted by those business circles that originally saw them as Bolshevism incarnate), they fell far, far short of the ideal of self-managed socialism. In essence, the workers were given the right to speak up on issues affecting their industry—which was a gain—but they got no power to make decisions. One of the consequences of genuine worker control (or even the illusion of that control) is that productivity goes up. But given the extremely limited nature of the workers' new rights—and the mood of "moroseness" that settled over the society not too long after the euphoria of May 1981—that pragmatic bonus from living up to an ideal was not forthcoming.

Third, the successful restructuring of companies wrecked by private management was a long-term proposition. In the short run, Mitterrand will probably be seen to have been much more competent than the French capitalists—but that was not exactly what the Socialists had in mind when they came to power. So it was that, by the middle of 1982, the soaring hopes that had accompanied the great legislative surge—not just nationalizations, but wage policy, the fifth week of vacation, early retirement and all the rest—ended, and the Socialist government adopted a policy of capitalist rigor. Or did it?

IV

The dramatic reversal in French Socialist strategy gathered momentum throughout the second half of 1982 and then became official policy in March 1983. That was, of course, precisely when the Reagan administration lucked into its demand-side recovery despite its supply-side policies. As it gradually became apparent that the American economy was on the move, and France under the Socialists was not only in retreat but stagnating, the contrast between Paris and Washington was all but chiseled in stone on both sides of the Atlantic. Indeed, Mitterrand's retreat was even read as a homage to Reagan's philosophy.

So it was that, in June of 1985, Jacques Chirac, who had launched an expansion quite similar to Mitterrand's in 1975, declared himself a born-again free enterpriser at a meeting of the opposition in Paris. There was a vogue among the intellectuals—as trendy and superficial as much of the leftism prior to 1981—for supply-side panaceas. Given the fact that, as the Bank for International Settlements so candidly recognized, Reaganomics does not apply in a second-rank economy with a vulnerable currency, one can expect widespread disillusionment on the right in the not-too-distant future if its campaign promises of 1986 are kept.

What is relevant is that, all the facile assertions of Mitterrand becoming a Reaganite notwithstanding, the French Socialists remained quite socialistic in retreat. That is, at every point they tried to defend the unemployed, the poorly paid, and the others on whose behalf they had so confidently acted in 1981. They made significant, even wrenching, concessions, particularly in their acceptance of economic firings, but they attempted to mitigate the effect of their own policies at every turn.

When the government hit the brakes on consumer spending in the spring of 1982 and declared a pay pause, the *smicards* were exempted from the new rules, and there were new taxes on income and wealth. They were, if truth be told, too modest to raise much revenue, but aggressive enough to make the rich even more surly, but I cite them to show that the basic Socialist values persisted, even if their application was not very effective. As the democratic Marxist, Alain Lipietz, put it, "the sacrifices demanded of households were characterized, *as far as their alloca-tion was concerned*, by considerations of social justice."

More broadly, the new tactics of 1982–83 did accept, but at the same time sought to minimize, more unemployment. Rather than simply allowing the jobless rate to soar and to reduce wages in that classic free-market fashion, the government adopted a program of controlled austerity. Wages were deindexed, which meant that their real value fell and profits absorbed all of the positive gains from productivity. But if the budget became more restrictive, there were also programs, borrowed from the Swed-ish Socialists, to create public-sector jobs, particularly for the youth. This whole strategy, not so incidentally, had been pro-posed from the Left by Serge-Christophe Kolm in an article pub-lished *before* the 1981 elections (and then developed at greater length in his book, *Sortir de la crise*).

Even more to the present point, the Socialists succeeded in their efforts! That is, if one departs from the 1980 levels of unem-ployment, then joblessness rose between 1981 and 1984 in France by 2 points, by 3.7 points in West Germany, and by 5.2 points in Britain. At the same time, the French growth rate was more stable than that of any other industrialized country during this period.

I do not cite these facts to sugarcoat the bitter pill of the Socialist failure. It is, however, of some moment that Mitter-rand's France outperformed Thatcher's Britain on just about every economic index of success, yet the Western, and particu-larly American, press was much more understanding of the prob-lems of Downing Street than of those in the Élysée. Moreover, one aspect of the French experience can be taken as a very em-pirical refutation of "supply-side" dogma: When the profits of French capital increased dramatically in 1984, investment stag-nated, not the least because the profits had risen as a result of holding down consumption.

But all of these qualifications, important as they are, are not the central lesson to be drawn from this chapter. François Mit-terrand proved that a decent and humane version of Keynes-ianism at the service of the poorest people in his society was not adequate to deal with the crisis of the eighties. In part, that failure was accentuated by the position of France—or, for that matter, of Europe—in the world market. Still, "Keynesianism in one country" is not possible, except for a brief period in the United States; the stimulation of mass consumption *within the old Fordist structures* will not yield the Fordist results of the fifties and sixties.

History, I believe, will be much kinder to the French Socialists than journalism has been and is. The point, however, is to learn from the mistakes and partial successes of François Mitterrand, so that the next Left will not be forced into an honorable, but humiliating, retreat.

7

Growth Through Justice

There is no question about whether the next several decades will be radical in character. That has already been decided. The question is which political forces—and values and ideas—will determine the shape of that radicalism.

The Reagan administration was the first American attempt to respond to this extraordinary new situation. The most ideological government in the history of the United States, it engaged in a vast experiment in "supply-side" economics that drastically redistributed income and wealth from the bottom and middle of the society and, at the same time and for that reason, incurred the largest federal deficits in the history of the nation.

Mr. Reagan himself was somewhat constrained by the realities of power and the fact that the electorate responded more to his personal charisma than to his announced program. But his supporters—and his possible heirs—were not subject to those limitations. As a result they have given full rein to their imagination, proposing ideas that are infinitely more audacious than anything emanating from the Left during the last decade or so.

Here, for example, is the "populist" Republican member of Congress from Georgia, Newt Gingrich—a major supporter of the supply-side leader, Jack Kemp. The president, Gingrich argues, should announce a "massive program" to build a lunar colony coupled with "a series of tax and regulatory incentives to turn space into a profitable arena for economic development." Are there right-wingers who are upset by this prescription for state intervention? "Conservatives who resist this government role," Gingrich remarks, "must be reminded that you cannot keep Panama Canals unless you first build them."

This rightist radicalism brings to mind an important proposition that was stated earlier: that the ideas of the Right and Left in this period will often bear a surface similarity that conceals a profound difference in fundamental values. Gingrich, for example, also makes a critique of the bureaucratic character of official medicine that might have been taken from a New Left document of the sixties. But his point is not to propose a more just, participatory system, but rather to attack government involvement in health as such.

The London *Economist* gives an even more compelling example of this phenomenon. "Between now and the next elections," it wrote in 1985, "the main political parties will be making much of their commitment to involve workers more closely in the businesses for which they toil." In fact, the *Economist* commented, the managerial concern with this issue is to find a way to get workers, under the guise of cooperation and joint decision making, to agree to accept sacrifices. "Many firms, having jumped on the participation bandwagon during recession, are now wondering how they can jump off."

Precisely because of "radical" attitudes on the Right that are actually ways of maintaining the status quo under new conditions, the programmatic alternatives of this chapter will not be simply "economic." Indeed, there is no such thing as an "economic" proposal in isolation from social and political considerations. Those who pretend to take such a neutral and technocratic point of view conceal a value-laden bias toward an authoritarian and elitist solution.

The Left should state its prejudices boldly. It is not just for resolving the present economic crisis, even though that is a precondition of everything else; it is for solving the crisis through an increase in freedom, in real popular control of the structures of society, very much including the new structures put forward by the Left. One of the secrets of the success of Fordism was that it united the drives for justice and efficiency, at least for a while. Now that must be done again, on an international level as well as within nations.

In trying to describe how this might be done, I will emphasize concepts rather than legislative proposals. For what the Left needs now is clarity in its basic orientations. If that can be achieved, if a political majority can be mobilized behind genuine new departures, there will be time to work out the details. In presenting these concepts in this chapter, I will focus on the United States, both because it is the country with which I am most familiar and because it is the decisive economy in the world. But I will refer freely to the European Left experience, and I assume that concepts that work in America have an application, after national modifications are made, in the Old World as well as the New.

Finally, my own analysis makes a certain humility imperative. Fordism did not come into existence as a result of a thought-through plan. The Swedish Socialists came closest to that model, but even in their case other factors were at work. And the New Deal was, as we have seen, an improvisation that was not even hinted at in Roosevelt's 1932 campaign.

I do not think that these ideas will chart the future. At best, like the immediate programs of Eugene Debs's 1912 Socialist campaign for the presidency that were adopted by the New Deal, they might make a contribution I cannot even anticipate. Even so, the possibilities imagined here are not the children of my wish but a response to the very specific history outlined in all that has gone before. They are a possible future suggested by my reading of the immediate past.

I

A central goal of the Left in the next generation must be the transformation of the meaning and character of work. That is not a utopian dream. It is a practical imperative if there is to be a just and efficient society under the unprecedented conditions of the final years of the twentieth century.

"Full employment" was once a liberal demand based upon the illusion that economic growth, in and by itself, would create jobs—what kind it did not matter—which would solve almost all social problems. For all of the flaws of that concept, it was a powerful idea that helped move the West from the catastrophe of the Great Depression to that Great Prosperity in which the average citizen made greater economic and social gains than at any time in human history.

One of the reasons that Western politics, including liberalism and social democracy, moved to the right during the past decade and a half is that the old notion of full employment was no longer achievable. That, however, does not mean that it is time to abandon the commitment to create work for all capable of doing it. That must remain a central value of the Left. What has to be understood, though, is that the full-employment goal of the late twentieth and the twenty-first centuries is, of pragmatic necessity, infinitely more radical and complex than the traditional Fordist demand of the fifties and sixties. More of the same work through the old model of growth is neither possible nor adequate for our social needs.

And yet, even though I share most of the criticisms of the traditional notion of full employment, I propose to use precisely that name in order to describe an agenda that goes far beyond anything it ever signified. My reasons are political, not rhetorical. There is an enormous resonance to the ideal of full employment among great masses of people in the West. It was not an accident, for instance, that the last campaign of Martin Luther King Jr. was for an Economic and Social Bill of Rights in which the very first right would be a constitutional guarantee of a job.

Since the politics of my rhetoric might cause some confusion—and since it is of critical importance for the Left to be clear on the meaning of full employment in the future as contrasted to the past—let me take some of the objections to the idea. The point is not to engage in a polemic, but to clarify the positive proposals that are being made in this chapter.

Claus Offe writes that full employment has been undermined by the very workings of capital itself: "The goal of absorbing the entire life energy of society into labor markets and industrial production has been rendered utopian." Therefore society needs "socially useful alternatives to the idea of full employment through wage labor." On the first count, I quite agree—which is why the concept of redefining the working life is so central to all that follows. The Left should look to a fundamental shift in the relation between free time and wage labor.

But does this mean that, *in the next historical period,* the Left should envision large numbers of able-bodied people who are completely outside of the world of wage labor? Is our proposal to detach the precarious poor, the unemployed, the rejected, from the system in which most of the people earn their daily bread? That is neither politically possible nor desirable.

The entire post–World War II period has demonstrated over and over that the "social wage," i.e., the income that people receive independent of their wage labor, can only rise in tandem with the compensation for wage labor itself. Simply put, those who have to get up in the morning and go to a job they do not particularly like will fight vigorously against any attempt to transfer an increasing portion of the production in which they engage to those who are outside of the system. And the reason for this attitude, it must be understood, is not that these people are selfish or egotistical, but that they rightly understand that many of their own needs are not being met. It is of some moment that the War on Poverty of the sixties was launched during a time in which the real income of the average citizen was going up regularly. Indeed, that was a precondition of the political viability of a proposal to be more generous with those who were not sharing in the advance.

We must, in short, make it economically possible for people to act upon their own best moral values. This point is not simply pragmatic. In his careful analysis of productivity and production trends, Edward Denison has computed that if the rates achieved in the growth period of 1948 to 1973 had prevailed from 1974 to 1982, then there would have been $1.4 *trillion* of additional output, measured in 1972 dollars (or roughly $3.6 trillion in 1982 dollars!).

Part of that enormous waste is the result of the chronic high rates of unemployment in recent years. Another part is a consequence of the fact that most of the new jobs generated in the last decade and a half have been in areas of low productivity. That is not simply an affront to the creative potential of the people in those occupations; it also squanders a most precious societal resource. That lost wealth, including the waste of human talent in menial work, would have financed wage increases, both private and social, and permitted the United States to take a much more just and decent attitude toward the Third World.

I say this even though I have long believed that the abolition of wage labor—that is, the creation of a society in which all work is voluntary because all basic needs are provided as a matter of right—is a desirable goal. One can agree or disagree with that socialist vision, but no one is so foolish to think that it can be placed on the political agenda in the foreseeable future. But to propose that *some people* begin to live such a utopia right now while the rest of the population is required to support them is not politically serious. What can and must be made a matter of practical debate is moving *everyone* a step closer to that ideal by a universal reduction in working hours.

Another objection to the concept of full employment comes from the very imaginative French thinker André Gorz. For Gorz, an old socialist dream—a dream of socialists who were artisans and skilled workers, for the most part—that people would find their emancipation *in* work has been totally subverted by the systematic deskilling of labor carried out by capital over the past century or so. Therefore the *only* liberation is to be sought in free time. That is partly true: Much of the work in Western society simply cannot be humanized under any conditions. But in part it is false: The new technology, if it is designed on the basis of emancipating social values (a critical point that will be expanded on shortly), could create new kinds of fulfilling work.

There are, after all, professionals and artists who already find personal enrichment in what they routinely do—and indeed there are many more of them than have ever existed before. We do not know to what degree that possibly can be expanded, but there is certainly potential there.

Then there are more immediate criticisms of the full employment ideal. Fred Block has shown that the amount of work available for people has been going down—leaving cyclical fluctuations aside—since 1910. At the same time in the seventies and the eighties, there was a rise in labor-force participation, most dramatically for women. Block concludes that "we have a situation in which we can anticipate less work and more people demanding a share of that work. Now in that context the slogan of 'full employment' becomes increasingly problematic."

Of course! Full employment is impossible if one accepts the present organization of the labor market as a given. What Block proves is precisely that full employment has become a radical demand. There is a related critique, articulated by Barbara Ehrenreich, among others. The new jobs of recent years, particularly those going to women and minorities, have been low-paid, menial, and without dignity. Isn't it therefore true that growth "determined according to capitalist priorities" will reinforce racial and gender discrimination? Again, of course! That is why I stress that the goal for the immediate future must be not simply to increase the quantity of work but to transform its character as well. That goal is not an attempt to use the occupational system to do social work; it is also a key to increased productivity in the next period.

Let me become much more immediate and less visionary.

It is clear that a central problem of every Western society in the eighties is the existence of a "subproletariat" of the unemployed, the precariously employed, the immigrants, and so on. Does one pension them off, see to it that their material needs are met, but leave them floating and functionless? Or does one understand, as the American Catholic bishops emphasized in their 1985 pastoral letter on the economy, that such an existence inevitably "marginalizes" human beings?

My answer is obvious. I believe that society in the future will be forced to go beyond the Protestant ethic, that belief that one's income and personal and social value are determined by a position in the paid labor market. But here and now, in the waning years of the twentieth century, a social version of the Protestant ethic is an absolute necessity for those at the bottom of Western society. They will not move from the economic underworld to utopia in a single bound, and if, by some political miracle they were able to do so, they would not know what to do with utopia. Their present lives, after all, have hardly schooled them in the ways of visionary living.

Full employment, then, is a practical necessity for the growing stratum of the marginalized, the precondition of their being able to lead meaningful lives. It is also one of the keys to a new surge of productivity in the service of, rather than at the expense of, the society.

II

The reduction of the working day and week is one of the ways to begin to implement the ideals I have just defined. But those measures, which must be placed on the immediate agenda of the Western Left, should also be seen as steps in the direction of a much more fundamental and distant goal: the redefinition of the working life.

The shorter workweek has an obvious quantitative potential: It can act as part of the strategy to create jobs for everyone by spreading the available work around. And it has a qualitative potential: to enrich people's lives with more free time, a process that, not so incidentally, has been one of the historic sources of increased productivity. But this concept is also more complex than it might at first seem. For it is true, as the Right says, that a sudden move to legislate a thirty-, or even a thirty-five-, hour week at forty hours' pay would most likely lead to economic crisis and radically reduced employment. And the briefest glimpse at just a few of the moments in the long history of this idea shows that there are other difficulties as well.

In the 1930s, for instance, there was a series of proposals to

cut back on working time. In the United States, many trade
unionists were opposed to work-*sharing*, to fewer hours at the
same pay (the major exception was in the needle trades where
the Amalgamated Clothing Workers—now the Amalgamated
Clothing and Textile Workers—have traditionally mandated
work-sharing). Still, the American Federation of Labor did support Senator (later Justice) Hugo Black's bill for a thirty-four-
hour week. And, to the consternation of President Roosevelt, his
own secretary of labor, Frances Perkins, came out for a thirty-
hour week.

Roosevelt shunted the Black bill aside and, in effect, sub-
stituted some vague promises in the National Industrial Recovery Act (NIRA) for it. In 1937, the National Recovery
Administration (the administrative body set up under the NIRA)
again reasserted the desirability of reducing the workweek but
not the weekly pay. But the NIRA was, of course, declared un-
constitutional and, in any case, in 1938 the forty-hour week was
finally established by law.

In 1939, the war orders began to pour into the American
economy and the Great Prosperity then removed the most urgent
incentive for considering a drastic shortening of the workweek.
The United Automobile Workers, however, did take up the issue
of working time. In 1976 it adopted a conscious strategy of seeking extra days off at every contract negotiation with the explicit
aim of forcing the companies to hire more workers and eventually
to be able to "trade in" the accumulated holidays for a four-day
week. But the crisis of the late seventies put an end to that tactic;
those paid days off were among the very first concessions exacted
from the union by the company.

In France, we have seen, the Popular Front of the thirties at
first did indeed create new job openings by cutting the workweek, but then ran into the hostility of capital and the shortage
of trained workers, and ultimately failed. Later on, in the
eighties, François Mitterrand was unable to redeem his bold
pledge for a thirty-five-hour week because most of the unionists
would not take a pay cut and, even in the euphoric days of 1981, it
was understood by the government that it could not increase the
wage bill in the private and public sectors by 12 percent. Among

many other consequences, that would have entailed making France even less competitive on the world market than it already was.

Both of these French cases are cited to prove that the idea of a radically reduced working time will simply not work. I read this history quite differently. It shows, rather, that, taken in isolation and leaving all the other limits of the system undisturbed, this proposal is not a panacea but a recipe for failure. But if one integrates this change into a larger plan that attends to those limits and moves them to the "left," I think it is of critical importance. So, in recent times, have the majority of trade unionists in Europe—women and men who are quite familiar with the French history of the thirties and eighties.

The fact of chronic high unemployment rates and the knowledge that the technological revolution was probably going to eliminate even more jobs led most of the unionists to campaign for the shorter workweek. In Germany, that strategy led to a bitter strike by the metalworkers, the largest single union in the country. Part of the idea was to reduce working time, not just in one nation, but in all of Europe. That would remove the competitive advantage of those economies with longer working weeks.

The Swedes were an exception to this consensus. They were very much for decreasing working time, but not as a means to achieve full employment. Other factors, such as productivity and profitability, determined the level of hiring, they said. And a sharp decrease in working hours, without a decrease in pay, would raise costs and make a country less competitive (a major consideration for Sweden, which is deeply involved in the world market). This critique has to be kept carefully in mind when we turn to the actual formulation of a concept of a shorter workweek.

On the other side, management has been busily going about the transformation of work for some time now. In 1985 the AFL-CIO reported that fully 20 percent of the people in the labor force were now part-time workers. Simultaneously, we have seen the emergence of both the underground economy and a sweatshop sector that, in the United States, preys on defenseless and fearful undocumented workers. In France, one of the most bitter disputes between management and labor has been over flexible hours. That is, the companies want to calculate the workweek on a yearly basis so that they are only charged overtime if the annual total of hours exceeds the annual maximum. In this way, workers can be forced to work long hours in some weeks without extra compensation so long as that is balanced out by weeks with short hours.

Here again, progressive ideas about much more flexibility in the allocation of labor time, which may, at first glance, seem far-fetched, are being turned into their opposite—like hiring more part-timers rather than regular workers—and put into reaction-ary practice by hardheaded businesspeople. That is one of the reasons why total hours per worker have been declining ever since the forty-hour-week law was passed. And it is a warning not to assume that a reduction in basic work time will automati-cally create new openings for the unemployed. That will only happen if hiring new people is more profitable than evading the law.

It is within this context that I propose realistic ways to cut the working day and week. The broad democratic Left should, once it has regained political power, set a target of the thirty-five-hour week.

As the French Socialist example so unfortunately proves, it is absurd to think that the employers of the United States will—or, to be fair, in some cases can—absorb the rapid increase in the hourly wage that would result from requiring them to pay forty hours worth of money for thirty-five hours of work. More broadly, the French example suggests that the Left *should avoid trying to redistribute income by means of the wage system*. That, as Mitterrand and company learned to their sorrow, acts as a disincentive to hiring people and, all other things being equal, leads to an increase in unemployment.

Assuming that the unions would voluntarily agree, the nation would proceed toward a thirty-five-hour week through a com-bination of collective bargaining (a part of the reduced time would be financed through normal increments in the wage but taken in this case in the form of increased leisure) and public subsidy. Since the Left should be committed to repealing the reactionary redistribution-of-tax burdens carried out by Reagan in the 1981 tax act, and continued in the 1986 tax law, that subsidy could take the simple form of a reduction in the tax burden of wage earners. Their total take-home pay for thirty-five hours would be at least equal to what they received for forty hours, but part of that increment would be financed through collective bargaining and part through the tax system.

But why should society pay for that tax subsidy? For reasons of tax justice, a subject that will be treated shortly; as part of the national commitment to full employment; *and* in order to increase productivity. The supply-siders, such as Jack Kemp, had based their philosophy on an old-fashioned, Fordist model when they argued that reduced taxes for working people would immediately raise productivity. In fact, the tax cut of 1981 was followed by a recession in which productivity declined for the usual reasons, and then followed by a recovery in which productivity did not increase in the usual way. But within a larger Left strategy to increase productivity, the Left might ironically accomplish what the Right had set out to do under Reagan.

Everything that has been said up until now about the reduction of the working week is realistic and sober. But the idea—and all the other very practical proposals that the Left must make—should also have a visionary dimension, for reasons that will become clearer in the next chapter.

One of the most moving accomplishments of the French Popular Front in the thirties was, through legislating vacation time, to make it possible for men and women who had lived in a country bounded by an ocean and a sea to actually visit the shore. And today, in talking about the workweek, the society should also debate the question of the working life. Why are sabbaticals reserved for academics? Wouldn't it make sense—and a social "profit"—to pay people to interrupt working in order to educate themselves? The "GI Bill of Rights" after World War II paid tuition, and a living and book allowance, to permit veterans to go to school. Wouldn't a civilian version of this policy have a similar yield in personal enrichment and enhanced productivity?

We know that, under Fordism, declining hours of work raised

productivity for the simple reason that the workers were no longer physically exhausted when they were on the job. But post-Fordism is a time when the gains in this area will derive more from raising the quality of work than from lowering its quantities. This visionary consideration points to a concept that has been referred to in passing but never really developed: the Left strategy for creating a new surge of productivity by means of an increase in social justice.

III

During World War II, there was probably more of an increase in social justice than at any time in American history. Wage and price controls were used to try to cut the differentials between the social classes; as over ten million men were drafted into uniform, blacks and women were brought into the factories and made the greatest relative gains before or since that time. There was also a powerful moral incentive to spur workers on: patriotism.

"According to conventional economic wisdom," Lester Thurow wrote in *The Zero Sum Solution*, "such efforts to promote fairness should have led to less efficient military production." In fact, there was a productivity explosion: an increase of 22 percent between 1940 and 1945. "To fight a war successfully," Thurow continues, "requires motivation, cooperation, and teamwork. They produce what might be called 'soft' productivity."

Indeed, it is a central theme of Thurow's important book that America's poor competitive performance on the world market vis-à-vis the Japanese and other nations "comes not so much from less 'hard' productivity (inferior technology) but from less 'soft' productivity (poorer motivation, less cooperation, adversarial relations rather than teamwork). *Soft productivity is an untapped productivity vein of gold.*" I have some disagreements with Thurow on other questions, but on this issue I think he has defined an essential aspect of the Left's strategy in the next period. Typically, sophisticated management has already grasped this point and, as usual, is coming up with its own manipulative version of a potentially progressive idea.

Thus, when Eastern Airlines was forced to make a deal with one of its unions, which gave the latter 25 percent of the stock in the company—and de jure seats on the board of directors—the president of the company immediately turned around and tried to use the new situation to break promises he had made to the workers as part of the deal. *Business Week*, as is often the case, was quite candid in this regard, in a glowing article on "the new corporate elite" in 1984.

The "organization man" is dead, *Business Week* asserted. Faced with the challenge of a radical new technology, entrepreneurs in small companies—"swashbucklers"—are antihierarchical, innovative, and even egalitarian. All of this, it should be obvious, is a rather romanticized vision of the Silicon Valley phenomenon written on the eve of a high-tech depression that was rather brutal with some of these myths. But what is particularly relevant here is the following very shrewd analysis: "Ironically . . . antiunion sentiment is the flip side of the new corporate elite's egalitarianism. With the exception of corporate rejuvenators who had inherited unions, virtually every one in the service and high-tech areas would do anything to keep organized labor out."

If all of this has a familiar ring, it is because it has happened before. The very first version of Fordism, the "welfare capitalism" of the twenties, sought to open up lines of paternalistic communication between management and workers precisely in order to keep the unions out. But if one understands the point cited in the *Economist*, that corporate enthusiasm for dialogue is usually a sure sign that the workers are being asked to give up something in return for "understanding," this is ominous.

More to the point, *there can be no enduring productivity gains based on the sham involvement of workers in the decision-making process.* To be sure, there can be—there have been—temporary advances in this area, but sooner or later, and sooner than many think, the manipulated see through the manipulation. Moreover, this kind of an authoritarian "democratization" as a result of corporate *noblesse oblige* could also lead to what Adolph

Sturmthal has called "joint paternalism," a gentleman's agreement between the company and its employees that promotes the privileges of both and the injustice of a "society of three speeds."

On every level, then, what is needed is genuine worker and community participation in basic decisions, like investment and plant location, which, under the Fordist social contract were declared to be the sovereign province of the corporate elite.

Let me begin with a fundamental issue that, though critical, can be resolved without radical change even though it is proposed as a step in that direction: worker participation in the *design* of technology.

There are those, I pointed out earlier, who naively think that technology is technologically determined. That is, the character of machines and the organization of work are seen as an engineering question to be decided by experts. In fact, as a growing library of research has demonstrated, technologies are the incarnation of values, of attitudes toward human beings. The "deskilling" of the labor force under capitalism, the drive to create a labor force reduced to the tending of the machines that essentially controlled the production process, was a hallmark of Fordism. More recently, as Harley Shaiken has documented, various computerized and robotized work processes have been consciously and explicitly designed in order to eliminate any influence on the part of potentially rambunctious men and women.

This is one of the reasons why the German labor federation, the DGB, demanded in 1985 that workers have the right to participate in all technological decisions. Similar proposals have been put forward by the machinists union (IAM) in the United States in a "technology bill of rights" for workers. The bricklayers, clothing workers, and ladies garment workers unions are all participating in joint efforts with management to create new technologies.

The next American Left should advocate, and pass, legislation *requiring* such an involvement of employees in technological decisions. And since the service and office sectors are increasingly high tech in character, that most emphatically includes them and not just factories or machine shops. But in urging this approach, one encounters a problem that is also a factor in every other proposal in this chapter: how to empower effective participation in decisions on the part of those who have been systematically excluded from them up until now.

In part that problem can be solved rather simply. The workers typically know much more than management about the work process. Indeed, one of the great sources of lost productivity in the United States—the capitalist country in which firing is easier than in any other—is that the people on the production line carefully hide their knowledge from the foreman out of fear that it will be used to increase output with fewer workers, i.e., to create unemployment.

In Japan, where male workers in major corporations have effective lifetime guarantees of employment, such knowledge can be shared with the company without harming those who figured it out. This is one of the forms of "soft" productivity that could be liberated through full employment. But the employees, whether in a factory or an office, do not have the spontaneous capacity to make arguments about technology—or any other traditional management—decisions. That involves sophisticated technical assessments of the interrelation between the work process, finance, markets, and the like.

So it is that in the outstanding cases where workers have achieved some measure of real participation in decisions, they have had the help of specialists in their dealing with the company. That is, they have had to develop a certain managerial expertise in order to participate in the debate that precedes the making of a decision. But then this is a problem for democracy in the age of bureaucracy and high tech generally, and it applies to communities fighting a decision of the government as well as to workers on the shop floor or in the office.

The next American Left should then announce a basic principle: government financial support to help those who want to fight government, or a private bureaucracy, to acquire the expertise to do so.

Absurd? Consider that, in the United States under the administration of Jimmy Carter (not a high watermark of American radicalism), there were concrete and successful actions along these lines. The Occupational Safety and Health Administration (OSHA) was under attack, sometimes justified, for its excessively bureaucratic approach to the absolutely necessary job of promoting safe conditions at work. Under two exceedingly imaginative administrators, Ray Marshall and Basil Whiting, OSHA decided not to hire staffers to monitor those safety conditions but to provide money to help unions develop their own competence to oversee their members' safety. The total cost was $10–$15 million a year, and the whole experiment was called off by the new Reagan administration in 1981. But the precedent is very significant.

There should be funds available to the rank and file in every walk of American life (and obvious qualifying rules can be established to exclude mere coffee klatches) who seek to challenge bureaucracies, be they private or public. And this would obviously apply with particular force to workers who are being empowered to participate in decision-making processes that have heretofore been the monopoly of management.

There is a larger social context in which this point operates, a sense in which the entire society has a stake in aiding particular groups to become effective participants in decision making. As two German socialist theorists, Johano Strasser and Klaus Traube, very well put it, the monopolization of professional competence is often more of an attack upon democracy than the open authoritarianism of the Right. For this gives a "technical" reason why the majority must obey and the experts must decide. It must be challenged.

German socialists are the source of another important idea: that the democratization of decision making should lead to different kinds of decisions. What is at stake is not just the *way* in which choices are made, but the choices themselves. Thus Johannes Rau, a major leader of German Socialism and quite possibly the future chancellor of his country, argued in 1985 for making ecological modernization a new growth industry. And that proposal had enormous political impact upon the electorate in a critical provincial election in 1985.

Similarly, the German Socialists have also argued that there may well be an entirely new future for cooperative enterprise in the advanced economies. That idea of a small factory controlled by its work force was one of the most primordial meanings of "socialism" in the nineteenth century. But then the Left realized that small-scale shops, which face-to-face cooperation and direct democracy require, were at a competitive disadvantage because they could not get the "economies of scale" that a giant corporation could achieve.

It was at this point that the European Socialists turned to the idea of nationalization, and the cooperative wing of the movement became distinctly secondary. Ironically, the most advanced twentieth-century technology now opens up the cooperative possibility. The famous enterprises of Silicon Valley are small and entrepreneurial and there is no reason why they cannot be run on a cooperative basis. And Charles Sabel has described small machine shops in Italy run cooperatively by skilled workers, most of them Socialists and Communists.

But perhaps the most radical departure suggested by the German Socialists has to do with working at home. Traditionally, the Left in general and the unions in particular rightly viewed that type of labor as socially dangerous. Hours cannot be regulated and neither can the toil of children. Moreover, it is impossible to organize a union of people dispersed in their own households. So "homework" was historically associated with the most cruel and exploitative forms of early capitalism.

But, the German Socialists argue, that is not *necessarily* the case. The idea that people leave their homes and travel long distances to work is, after all, a relatively recent development and there is much to be said for ending the practice. Doing so would, among other things, economize on the time and money spent in commuting, and even make new forms of urban planning—or decentralized communities—possible.

The crucial question here would be, Is it possible for society to regulate such activities, to see to it that they are not the agency of a deunionization of the labor force that leaves the individual at the mercy of a boss who appears in the form of a command on a computer screen? Here again, one and the same concept—working at home—can be effectuated in an extremely progressive or an extremely reactionary way. It could be the basis of a more decentralized society or of a "1984" in which the television and computers monitor the lives of utterly fragmented and alienated people.

But what do all these ideas, perhaps good, perhaps bad, have to do with the claim of this section that there is a new vein of productivity to be mined? The case of Eastern Airlines is extremely interesting in this regard.

In 1983, Frank Borman, the president of Eastern, was publicly hinting that his company would have to go into bankruptcy if it did not get major concessions from its unions. To the surprise of the latter—the IAM, the Air Line Pilots Association, and the Association of Flight Attendants—Borman even gave them access to the company books in an attempt to persuade them that they had to make major concessions if Eastern, and their jobs with it, was going to survive.

By this time, the unions, under the leadership of District 100 of the machinists, had developed considerable expertise and they had the help of a labor consultant, Randy Barber, who specializes in precisely such matters. Borman was then amazed to discover that the unions had used their access to inside information to document how the company was giving two different reports on its conditions: a pessimistic analysis for the unions that were supposed to make concessions; an optimistic account for the banks and other sources of possible funds. At the end of 1983, Eastern and the unions agreed that some $295 million in wage concessions would qualify the workers to receive 25 percent of the Eastern stock and thus to take up a powerful minority position on the board of directors.

In the first year of the contract, there were productivity savings of $472 million! One machinist, for instance, suggested a way of rewelding discarded heat shields, which saved $304,000. In a second contract, the company agreed that the workers could "buy back" their own concessions by making productivity increases. Two years after this innovative bargain was made, the machinists at Eastern were the highest paid in the industry— but the company's labor costs were still low because of the productivity increases. There is a similar story in Philadelphia where a union bought out the O & O supermarket.

Alas, an extremely important caveat now has to be emphasized. Attempts to give the rank and file real voice in the decision-making process are subject, not simply to the resistance of management, but to the constraints imposed by the very structure of the economy. This is a specific case in point of a broader proposition that I alluded to earlier: that the reforms of the Left always take place on the terrain of the Right, i.e., they must modify, but also operate within, a system that is hostile to them.

In the labor negotiations of 1985–86 at Eastern, the company insisted on new sacrifices that, it said, were mandated by the economic situation. As a result of the deregulation of the airline industry and the emergence of a number of low-cost carriers, Eastern, even with the productivity gains of recent years, was, its president said, at a competitive disadvantage. He did not, of course, add that part of the problem was due to serious management errors in the seventies with regard to upgrading an aging fleet of planes. But if the unionists were quite right to be skeptical about many of the details of the economic "necessity" invoked by management—historically such necessity has the most remarkable congruence with what management wants to do anyway—it was not a pure fiction by any means.

Unfortunately, at this writing the whole Eastern experience is in a kind of limbo. The airline has been sold to Francesco Lorenzo, a man who has compiled a notable antiunion record at Texas Air and Continental. The stock rights and seats on the board of directors remain as negotiated, yet it is quite possible that the new management will be hostile to the whole idea. That only reinforces the point that such innovations in ownership and decision making cannot be undertaken in isolation.

It is true that, even where there is effective worker participation (or, for that matter, worker ownership), the imperatives of a hostile economy have a voice in the boardroom that can be louder than that of management or of the workers. Therefore it is important to see economic democracy, not as an individual or local collective, but as a part of a national effort to change the trends of the economy itself. If that is not done, then the rank and file have only won the right to discipline themselves. One European case points in the direction of situating workers' control in a larger social context. It is, I must admit, an ambivalent example.

The idea of "wage-earner funds" originated in the blue-collar labor federation, LO, and was formulated by one of its chief economists, Rudolf Meidner (the German Socialists had considered a similar proposal in the early seventies but abandoned it because of opposition from their partners in a coalition government).

In the early formulations, the concept was quite radical. Companies would have to pay an excess-profits tax to a worker-controlled mutual fund that would then invest the money into collectively owned and managed stock that would entitle the workers' representatives to seats on the board of directors. In this form, the funds would have been a way of creating decentralized social ownership, which would eventually control the commanding heights of the Swedish corporate economy. The Swedish Socialists, it must be remembered, had nationalized less than 5 percent of the economy during forty-four years in power. This was a significant new departure.

In the mid-seventies, when the issue of the funds first became a matter of fierce debate in Sweden, the argument for them was not simply based on wage considerations. The funds were seen as a way to countervail the very high degree of corporate concentration in Sweden, as a step toward workers' control and as an incentive to capital formation. On that last count, it was said that workers who actually had a say in, and even received benefits from, profits would be much more likely to forgo wages in the name of raising capital than workers who were simply the hired hands of capital.

Swedish business was outraged. It treated the funds, which were decentralist and democratic, as if they heralded the coming of the Stalinist gulag. That campaign was successful among the population as a whole, and even Socialist voters were often negative about the reform. As a result, the Socialist party retreated. There would be a wage tax as well as a profits tax; the funds would be regional with community representation; and, most important, no fund, or even coalition of funds, could buy more than 8 percent of the stock in a given corporation.

It is possible—I would say, it is to be hoped—that eventually the funds will get back some of the original, and more radical, features. But even in their present form—and the monies for them will cease to come in at the end of the decade—they stand for an extremely important principle. The workers' ownership they create is collective, not individual. The idea of "profit sharing," which has had a certain vogue in the United States at various times, makes the workers into individual owners of small amounts of stock, i.e., makes them as irrelevant to the managerial decision-making process as any other small stockholder. The Swedish funds, even in their modified version, empower a new and active partner in the making of decisions within the corporation.

The contrast with the United States is quite instructive. Under the law, Washington gives tax preferences to Employee Stock Ownership Plans (ESOPs). That idea was developed by Senator Russell Long in order to promote capitalism among the rank and file of the work force, not to change the relations of power and decision. When the crisis hit in the seventies, not a few corporations saw that the moment offered an opportunity, not simply to get concessions out of their work force, but to do so with government subsidy. So in return for giving up wages and benefits, the workers were given "ownership" rights under the ESOP provision.

In most of these cases—Eastern Airlines is a notable exception—the concessions were real, the "ownership" a fraud without any rights to intervene in anything, and the special treatment from the government was worth money. As an official at the Department of Labor put it in 1985, "A lot of ESOPs are really MESOPs—management-entrenchment or management-enrichment stock ownership plans."

Thus, one of the very first—and simple—things an American Left in power should do is to rewrite the law to provide for real, collective, decision-making power wherever there is a government subsidy for a stock-ownership plan. And that can be urged, not merely as a matter of basic equity for the workers involved, but also as part of a national productivity policy that seeks to advance the entire economy through the practical gains that can be made through democratization.

The Left must always prove that it is not woolly and utopian in the worst sense of the word, and I have therefore emphasized the "hard"—realistic, profit-making—arguments for the proposals of this section. Ultimately, the American Left would do well to also adopt the basic commitment to the democratization of the economy put forward by the Catholic bishops in their 1985 pastoral letter. It has become necessary to be more idealistic, to translate the profound American commitment to political democracy into a new program for economic and industrial democracy.

There is a corollary to that proposition and it is not always understood by the college-educated Left. In the thirties and forties, all middle-class progressives were, as a matter of course, prolabor. The unions were, after all, *the* great social insurgency. But then as early as the fifties, there was a certain breakdown in this attitude as reformers began to look upon unions as just another institution among many. And that suspicion often turned into outright hostility when the Meany wing of the AFL-CIO became the staunchest supporter of a Vietnam intervention overwhelmingly opposed by students, civil rights militants, and feminists. The new social insurgencies came into conflict with the old.

In the seventies and early eighties that situation ameliorated somewhat. As conservative power grew, a number of the college-educated activists began to realize that unions in general, and the progressive unions that had fought against the war in Vietnam in particular, could be important allies in various struggles. Still, there was often an air of the pragmatist pursuing the lesser evil in this new commitment on the part of the middle-class Left.

So it must be made clear that any hope for economic democracy depends not simply on the maintenance of the American unions but upon their dramatic expansion in the service sector— among clericals, and among women and minorities in particular. In immediate political terms, that must mean a renewed battle for labor-law reform. As noted earlier, the Canadian unions grew while the United States unions declined, in considerable measure because Canadian law facilitates rather than frustrates labor organization.

More broadly, the Left that has been rightly sensitive to the social movements of minorities, women, and gays and lesbians has to once again understand that the class-based movements of the workers are not simply concerned with economics but are themselves, in fact or potentially, social movements seeking to change the very conditions of daily life. Without a renewal of trade unionism, most of the ideas urged here are impossible.

IV

Tax policy is another area where the Western Left can link justice and efficiency as it moves beyond Fordism.

During the heyday of Fordist growth, the issue of "fair shares" was effectively removed from the political agenda. It was the received wisdom of Fordism that growth was much more important than distribution. (That the neoconservatives now totally falsify this reality, attacking the Keynesians for being obsessed with distribution is just one more example of the convenient rewriting of history.) The Kennedy-Johnson tax cuts were much more progressive than those initiated by Ronald Reagan, but they did contain handsome subsidies for capital.

This lack of concern with the distribution of income and wealth was much more marked in the United States than in Europe and Canada. In those welfare states, Socialist and Social Democratic influence saw to it that the social wage was made available in universal programs without a means test. In the United States, the nonaging poor were subjected to humiliating restrictions that often had the effect of keeping them from getting benefits.

At the same time, many elements of the social wage were implemented through tax-subsidized fringe benefits—health care is the most obvious example—which provided generous coverage, *so long as the job lasted*, for the best organized and nothing for the unorganized. Ironically, as Lester Thurow has shown, the lower wages in the Japanese auto industry are the result of the high charges for fringe benefits in American auto production. Were there a system of national health in this country, the Japanese margin would all but disappear!

Then Ronald Reagan put redistribution back on the political agenda. On the basis of a spurious capital-shortage theory, the

1981 tax act drastically redistributed wealth from the poor, the working people, and the middle class to the upper middle class and the rich. At the same time, the social wage of the poor was reduced, by inflation as well as by budget cuts. The conservative head of the Congressional Budget Office testified that the real value of food stamps and AFDC in the early eighties was less than the worth of AFDC alone in the late sixties.

Using the fraudulent argument that excessive government spending was the cause of the economic crisis, Reagan mesmerized the Democratic party into accepting his basic rationale. Thus in 1981, the Democrats in Congress *competed* with the Republicans in creating new giveaways for the rich and the corporations. In the congressional debate on tax reform in 1985 and 1986, the Democrats did succeed in making the law more progressive than the one Reagan proposed, and yet they still accepted the proposition that the whole process had to be "revenue neutral," i.e., that there be no basic attempt to cut the deficit by requiring that the rich pay their fair share of the burden.

The Left should respond to the Reagan—and Thatcher— challenge and put *progressive redistribution* back on the political agenda.

At the same time, I assume that the lesson taught in France is plain enough by now. One should not attempt to redistribute through either wages or payroll taxes, since sharp increases in both create employment disincentives in an economy that is going to be substantially private for the foreseeable future (and in which the public sector is subject to most of the constraints that operate with the private corporations).

In a sense, the American case is the easiest to deal with, since its labyrinth of tax inequities is worse than that of any other Western country. The Left should campaign to take away all the handouts to the rich contained in the 1981 tax act; more broadly, to remove every subsidy to capital that does not have a proved job-generating impact; to revise the 1986 law so as to tax the private income and wealth of the affluent as a major source of funds and social justice.

There are many innovative ideas that might be considered in this regard. For instance, Hyman Minsky and others have suggested that the corporation tax, much of which is passed along to the consumer, be abolished. Then the undistributed profits of corporations should be prorated to the owners of stock and calculated as part of their income. There would no longer be the famous "double taxation of dividends" (once in the corporate tax, a second time in the income tax of those who receive the dividends) so abhorrent to the Right. But neither would there be a form of income and wealth—the appreciation in the value of corporations—that is not taxed when it occurs and is therefore a prime target for total avoidance.

At the same time, full employment would make it possible to create an adequate social wage for those unable to work—or those whose retraining or even leisure time was regarded as socially valuable and worthy of support. Indeed, some of the most important feminist proposals for dealing with the fact that women who work in the paid labor market almost always must perform a second job in the unpaid, domestic labor market could now be placed on the table. Day care, provisions for paternity leave to allow fathers to share with mothers the care of infants, and social-wage support for women who choose to work only in the unpaid labor market at home are just a few of the ideas that would then become relevant.

So is the idea of a children's allowance. It exists throughout Europe and in Canada and, as in the case of national health, the United States and South Africa are the only "advanced" economies that lack it. AFDC is an utterly inadequate program with enormous variations on a state-to-state basis and considerable potential for bureaucratic interference in the lives of recipients. The lives of children and parents would be bettered if there were a universal system of allowances for *all* children, which would provide an income floor for all forms of parenting. That grant would be taxable, i.e., though universal it would, in effect, be taxed away in the case of those families that had no need for it.

These various redistributive policies, it must be noted again, are also linked to promoting efficiency. The Japanese, Lester Thurow has documented, have about half the income inequality of the United States. Worse, there is abundant evidence that income inequality in the United States is increasing, even though it does not perform any economic function. A study by Bennett Harrison, Chris Tilley, and Barry Bluestone, published by the Joint Economic Committee in 1986, showed that the inequality in salaries and wages had grown by 20 percent between 1978 and 1985. A study of poverty by the Congressional Research Service in 1985 found the same trend—but located its beginning in 1968—and saw it as a major cause for the tremendous increase in the number of children who are poor.

It was a basic dogma of the conservatives, such as Reagan and Thatcher, who took over in the wake of the collapse of liberal and socialist Fordism, that inequality is good for production. The record simply does not bear out this self-serving ideology of the rich, since the society became less equal in good times as well as bad in recent years, in considerable measure because the Right promoted that trend. Therefore one of the essential tasks of the next Left will be to reestablish, in imaginative ways, the historic fact that increases in social justice are the very best stimulus for increased production.

All of the proposals in this chapter can only be accomplished if they are done within the framework of democratic planning.

That statement is potentially misleading. More often than not, discussions on the Left have ended with a call for planning as if the very idea itself were both radical and obvious. In fact, every single economy in the modern world, from the most centralized, Stalinist-type Communist society to the most vociferous free-market nation, is in fact planned. Planning is inevitable in the late twentieth century and it can be the instrument of the Right and the Center as well as the Left. Therefore, when I talk about *democratic* planning in this section, the reference is to something that is both distinctive and utterly new.

In the United States under Ronald Reagan, the government lends, or guarantees, $1 trillion, which, as Lester Thurow points out, makes it our leading investment banker. Those who think that decisions about such a huge sum of money do not affect "free" markets have not noticed the world around them. In 1961, chips for integrated circuits cost $120 a piece; in 1971, $2. That triumph of capitalist productivity was achieved via a guaranteed market under the space program, which allowed private corporations to explore solutions without having to depend upon the vagaries of supply and demand.

For that matter, the centerpiece of Ronald Reagan's first administration, the Economic Recovery Tax Act of 1981, the central exercise in "supply-side" economics, was a planner's scheme, not the dictate of a market. Reagan and company had wrongly determined that, because of government interference through excessive welfare-state spending, the capital markets were not providing enough investment funds for the private sector. They decided to correct this "lamentable" situation—by further government interference.

The planners' goal was announced explicitly in the 1982 Report of the Council of Economic Advisors: "The Administration seeks to increase capital formation by both raising the level of output and reducing the fraction of output consumed. . . . Thus to achieve higher national saving rates it is important to lower the household consumption rate." How is this purpose to be accomplished? By totally deregulating financial markets and letting the citizen's personal—and completely private—choice set the mix of consumption and saving? That would be the solution of a Hayek. It was not the solution of Ronald Reagan.

The Council of Economic Advisors was quite candid in this regard. "Household choices between consumption and saving and between work and leisure," it wrote, "are influenced by after-tax wage rates and after-tax rates of return on capital. When the *government* changes either the level or the structure of taxes, it ultimately alters household decisions about consumption, saving, and work effort." (emphasis added) Note: the *government* was going to make the basic decision by creating a tax environment in which the citizen would "freely" make the decision the government wanted.

Indeed, the very first experiments in national economic planning were all made by moderate to conservative governments during World War I when they mobilized their societies behind the war effort. There is a common thread that runs from the American War Industries Board of 1917—dominated by corporate planners—through the Reconstruction Finance Corporation initiated by Herbert Hoover and taken over by Franklin Roosevelt, to the proposal made by the investment banker Felix Rohatyn for a new government investment bank when the crisis hit in the seventies.

It was no accident that Rohatyn's idea attracted a considerable number of sophisticated businessmen precisely during the recessions of 1974–75 and 1981–82, i.e., in bad times, and then disappeared from policy discussion as soon as the economy improved. Just as in the case of corporate fascination with "worker participation" as a way to get sacrifices made when profits are low, such high-minded thoughts about planning are abandoned as soon as the business climate improves. There is, in short, rightist planning, centrist planning, and, quite distinctively, the planning of the Left.

The latter, it must be emphasized, is not simply concerned with democratic procedures, though they are certainly a precondition of progress. It also seeks a social and democratic *content*. It is, I think, no accident that, when Rohatyn's model of technocratic, elite planning was applied to solve the New York City crisis in the mid-seventies, commuters had to pay higher fares, public employees were laid off, students were forced, for the first time in history, to pay tuition at the City University, and the banks, which dominated the planning process, were not required to give up anything. Only the naive will be surprised to learn that this distribution of burdens was made under the direction of a bankers' committee committed, of course, to "equality of sacrifice."

So the Left is for truly democratic procedures for the planning it advocates because, among many other considerations, that is the only way to make substantially democratic outcomes possible. But then, a point made earlier about worker participation in management decisions takes on an even greater relevance. In contemporary society, the average citizen or community is simply not prepared to engage in the *technical* debate over how to implement a basic policy.

People know what they want. But they cannot translate their desires into a planner's language. That is why I have long believed that the government must provide funds so that the communities at the base can hire their experts and computer time and engage in counterplanning as against government or corporate bureaucrats. In an excellent book, *Habits of the Heart*, Robert Bellah and his coauthors read this notion as evidence of an insufficient commitment to the rule of the rank and file, as an unnecessary concession to the experts and their technocratic ideology.

I disagree. The planning process must utilize all of the scientific and technical tools now at our disposal, and the people do not spontaneously understand these matters, even if they are quite clear about the values they want to implement. It is clear that the experts who would be hired by a community or a union could take over the whole process in the name of their superior knowledge. It is also true, as some of the examples I have already given of successful union buy-outs have shown, that the ranks can make the experts their servants, too. I see no alternative to accepting this challenge.

The key to democratic planning should be the creation of a full employment economy. That, as the next section will make clear, has an international dimension, but for now I will focus on the concept as it operates within a national framework.

Thus, the problem posed to the planners, national and local, will be: What must be done to achieve full employment? Then, following the broad outlines that were spelled out in the original Humphrey-Hawkins bill of the early seventies (which was watered down into the unenforced—and unenforceable—Humphrey-Hawkins Act of 1978), Washington should be required to state precisely what kind of government intervention is necessary to achieve that goal in the next year or planning period. In detailing the measures to be submitted to Congress for that purpose, the government should be required to rely on a national-needs inventory, which will involve local planning groups with competent staffs stating their priorities.

There is obviously no point here in trying to write a bill, but at least three areas of possible action deserve to be noted. First, there should be a concerted attack on the tax-subsidized waste of the private corporate sector. Contemporary capitalism, which speaks in the mythic tones of entrepreneurial innovators, has become welfare-dependent and gets enormous public support for the "casino society" of economically useless, or harmful, speculation. For instance, a 1986 cover story by *Business Week* described "The Hollow Corporation." "A new kind of company is evolving in the U.S.—manufacturing companies that do little manufacturing. Instead, they import components of products from low-wage countries, slap their own names on them and sell them in America. Unchecked, this trend will ultimately hurt the economy—retarding productivity, innovation, and the standard of living."

So there should indeed be tax subsidies for private corporations that create jobs in areas of high unemployment and poverty, but those subsidies should be given after the fact, on the basis of accomplishment rather than of vague promises. And not a penny should go to the "hollow corporations."

Secondly, a full-employment agenda will involve the enlargement of the public sector, if only because business has demonstrated itself to be totally unwilling to make necessary investments in areas of social need. We must, for instance, examine the feasibility of creating new regional rail systems under decentralized public ownership. That could create a service that would pay for itself and open up a large number of jobs.

For a variety of reasons, the goal of creating a national health system in the United States must be placed back on the agenda. Workers who have lost their jobs, we have seen, also lost their health coverage under the contract. The new shape of the labor force, with its great concentration of women and minorities in low-paid, unorganized jobs with minimal fringe benefits (and, in the case of part-time workers, with no fringe benefits at all), is creating an entire stratum of the medically needy. At the same time, corporate organization and profit making are taking over the health system in a frightening way and hospitals committed to the care of the poor are being overwhelmed by all of the "non-profitable" cases they get as a result. And costs have, of course, soared, as the United States has built a system that is not only socially irresponsible but incredibly expensive at the same time (this country devotes more of a percentage of its GNP to health than any of the nations with national health systems!). Private fee-for-service medicine financed by third-party insurers has brought the worst of both capitalism and socialism to the U.S.

The growth of health maintenance organizations (HMOs) and an oversupply of doctors give a certain political opening to change this cruel and inefficient system. So does the fact that, in 1986, a Reagan administration commission came up with an eminently socialist proposal with regard to organ transplants. Since the organs are gathered as part of a communal effort, the commission said, issues of life and death should not be determined by income or wealth, and this care should be provided without cost to the patient. The commission did not notice that all of the rest of the health system does indeed ration life and death on the basis of the purse. The Left should notice, for this is an area in which full-employment planning can maximize human service for the entire society—and save money at the same time.

The public sector can also play a significant role in relationship to the private sector. Hyman Minsky has shrewdly advocated abolishing minimum-wage legislation—which is poorly enforced, if at all, in these days of the sweatshop—and substituting guaranteed jobs for it. If, for example, federal policy provided work for anyone who wanted it at, say, $7 an hour, no private employer would be able to pay less. The traditional argument against such a policy is that if one thus lifts wages above their (mythical) "market" level, that motivates employers to substitute machines for people. That is obviously true if, but only if, one merely raises the minimum wage and does nothing else. But if we understand that in the framework of a shorter workweek and a planned fulfillment of social needs, we actually *need* people to do quality jobs, that objection falls by the way. A nation should rejoice in the destruction of menial occupations if that means that the people who once held them can now do more economically and socially useful work.

Third, planning should not require that obsolete technologies and industries be maintained in place. But it should work to see to it that the transition from one technology or industry to another should not be made at the expense of the workers and their communities. In doing so, corporations should be made to pay their fair share of the social costs of their private decisions, and there should be an effective commitment to provide displaced workers with jobs as good as, or better than, the ones that are being phased out of existence. Here, too, a commitment to social justice should promote productivity, since workers with such assurances would not be fearful of sharing their own knowledge about improving the production process or be forced to resist technological change in general.

Finally it should be clear by now that, even though some of the early drafts of the Humphrey-Hawkins bill can be used for important ideas on how to proceed, what is being urged here is not a return to the ideas of the sixties and the early seventies. The goal for the future—full employment—is the same as it was then. But the means to effect that goal, even though they are still found within the framework of the mixed economy, are more radical than anything the sixties or seventies ever considered.

VI

The international strategy of the next Left should have the same essential point as the national: to link justice with efficiency, but this time on a global basis.

Let me immediately admit that, difficult as it is to follow that approach within a single country, it is infinitely more complex when one tries to internationalize it. Many countries in Africa are still struggling to achieve a national consciousness, and most of them do not possess the infrastructure to do sophisticated planning. That such problems are the ugly heritage of Western domination, a part of the crime of imperialism, does not make them any less real. In Latin America, even after some of the extraordinary gains made by democracy in recent years, there are still powerful oligarchies, antidevelopmental attitudes, and not a little corruption. In Asia, despite the fact that the population is not increasing as fast as once feared, sheer numbers are an enormous problem.

So if I make analogies with the Marshall Plan—and I do—they must be carefully qualified. It is one thing to provide capital for European economies that have been through the capitalist cultural and technological revolution and thereby to overcome the temporary problems of war devastation. It is another thing to seek to help countries leap centuries into modernity and to avoid both totalitarian capital accumulation or a fundamentalist reaction to change of the kind that occurred in Iran.

But these sobering considerations should not keep us from taking first steps toward global justice—steps that will help the North as well as the South solve its problems. The basic analysis behind the concepts that will be briefly set forth here has been worked out in the two volumes of Willy Brandt's Independent Commission on International Development Issues, *North-South* (1980) and *Common Crisis* (1983), and by the report of the Socialist International Committee on Economic Policy chaired by Michael Manley of Jamaica, *Global Challenge* (1985).

But didn't Mitterrand, who quite consciously followed Brandt's lead in his 1981 attempt to engage in "planetary Keynesianism," show that the idea will not work at all? I think not. He did prove that a second-rank economy, acting in isolation in the midst of the worst recession in half a century, cannot radically change a global structure that is the work of some centuries of injustice. However, were the United States to take the lead, enlisting Europe and Japan in the undertaking, and appealing to the advanced Communist countries as well, there is good reason to believe that there could be an international marriage of justice and efficiency.

After all, as chapter 4 showed, the Marshall Plan did indeed benefit the United States as much as it did the recipient nations. The grants and loans created jobs in the American economy to build the machines and factories that were the basis of the reindustrialization of Europe and Japan. And if I have already admitted that this analogy is somewhat faulty, the recycling of petrodollars by the Western banks in the mid-seventies was a relative success, undercut by both the crisis of Fordism itself and the second oil shock.

But then the most startling confirmation of this optimistic analysis comes from the International Monetary Fund, the very citadel of "realism" in such matters, and the Reagan administration itself.

As the managing director of the IMF, J. de Larosière, put it in the late seventies, "It is paradoxical that the industrialized countries, most of which are not using their production potential to the full, are hesitating to increase their financial aid to poor countries. This is despite the fact that such aid could result in increased global demand and thus would contribute to reactivation of world trade in a recovery of production."

But then, one need not be content with speculations about what might have happened in the seventies, for there are important lessons to be drawn from what did in fact happen. It was bad economics as well as bad morality in the decade when the nations reduced their official aid and let the banks take over the job of recycling petrodollars. It was also stupid for the banks to follow the lead of Walter Wriston of Citibank and to adopt the "sovereign risk hypothesis" that nations never go bankrupt and therefore the most questionable loan is defensible. That was, and is, a major source of the world debt crisis of the eighties. And it is one of the continuing outrages *within* the Third World that so much of the money received from Western banks in the seventies was sent back to those very same banks by the rich in the poor countries rather than being invested in economic development.

But having made all these qualifications, it is true that the bank lending worked. Between 1973 and 1981, economic growth in the industrial countries declined to 2.8 percent—and held steady in the Third World at 5.1 percent. Indeed, the markets created by that growth in the Third World were an important reason why the decline in the developing countries was not even greater. If the transfer of funds from North to South thus succeeded under some of the worst conditions imaginable, there is a very realistic argument that such a shift could have a positive effect when it is a function of a multinational and governmental plan rather than an accidental byproduct of go-go banking.

These realities have even infiltrated the conservative mind.

In 1982, when the threat of Mexican default opened up the possibility of a catastrophic world financial crisis, the Federal Reserve Bank admitted, in deeds if not in so many words, that such a collapse would be profoundly detrimental to American self-interest. After all, at that point world debt stood at a sum twice as great as the total reserves of the ten largest banks in the United States. Had a chain reaction of bank failures been set off in the midst of a deep recession, there was no telling what the consequences would be.

And even though a global money crunch was avoided, the crisis of the early eighties had a profound impact upon the advanced economies. In 1985, *Business Week* reported that the crisis in the South, particularly in Latin America, had lost exporters in the United States $18 billion between 1980 and 1984 and had cost workers one million jobs. Considerations like these were certainly a factor in the decision of Reagan's treasury secretary to call for more money for the debt-ridden economies at the 1985 meeting of the IMF.

James Baker was not being a liberal but a sophisticated conservative. There was proof of that fact in his proposal. He wanted the World Bank and the governments that fund it to underwrite a small portion of the Third World debt payments. But he did not suggest actually reducing the debt itself or retreating from the disastrous reliance on private banks. What was significant is that his utterly inadequate proposals, which also included more than a little mandatory Reaganism for the recipient nations, were based on the recognition of the fact that the North is dependent upon the South and not just vice versa.

The sophisticated moderates were better than Baker. Senator Bill Bradley of New Jersey urged a reduction in interest rates for the Third World and a consequent cut in the debt itself. And a 1986 editorial in the *New York Times*, headlined "The Rich Must Lend or Wither," rightly argued that "funds prudently lent to third-world countries would flow back in demand for manufactured exports [in the United States], helping the very industries that now suffer most from a chronic overcapacity."

"Private banks," the *Times* editorial continued, "can't do that job. They are saturated with foreign debt and preoccupied with minimizing their losses to the heavy debtors of the 1970s."

The Left should, I believe, go well beyond the moderates and conservatives, proposing a multinational program of global growth, North and South, to be run by governments, not banks; to include the Soviet Union; and to refrain from imposing American economic panaceas on the Third World, not only because they are normally irrelevant to the history and structure of that region, but also because they are failing here. That program should also accept the proposition, first made by Peru's Socialist president, Alan Garcia, that no developing nation should ever be required to pay interest in excess of a manageable percentage of its export income. For the austerity economics of the International Monetary Fund, which demands that countries impoverish their people in order to meet their obligations to foreign banks, is not simply cruel but a prescription for world economic disaster as well.

So the key concept of the Left's international economic program must be this: *that a transfer of money and technology from North to South will put the people of the North to work creating more justice in the South and, of course, create jobs in the South at the same time.*

There are two related concepts. First, it is clear that disarmament, nuclear and conventional, is an absolute imperative for all societies in the final years of the twentieth century. It is not just that the superpowers have the capacity to blow up the planet, which is bad enough. For even if that does not happen, one of the most disgraceful facts of recent international life is the way in which Northern suppliers have found a huge market for their sophisticated weapons of "conventional" destruction in Third World countries that are still struggling for the basic means of survival.

The Left should therefore propose that part of the funds that would be saved by big-power governments as a result of disarmament be earmarked for economic development in the South through multinational institutions. That last qualification is necessary to keep the wealthy nations from spending all of that money according to military priorities, which is what they normally have done.

And secondly, this whole approach could radically change the attitude of workers in the North, many of whom see the workers of the South as people who are trying to take their jobs away by toiling for what are, by advanced capitalist standards, starvation wages. If this proposal were made within the context of the full-employment commitment I have just described, and if the workers of the West saw that economic and social justice in the poor countries was in their own material interest, that could very much change the politics of the developed countries for the good.

It is extremely hard to imagine such a change in the very structures of the world itself—harder even than seeing the possibility of linking justice and efficiency within a single nation. And yet, just as the failure to act nationally will create a "society of three speeds" in the advanced economies, a retrogression from whatever advances have been made in the course of more than a century of popular struggles, the inability to act internationally will create a world that is not only monstrously unjust but terrifying in its instability as well.

Moreover, all of these proposals, national and international, can be summarized in terms of the radical project that has become a practical necessity: to push the limits of welfare-capitalist society to the left. In the analysis of the Mitterrand experience, it was apparent that trying to make basic revisions of societal priorities within the framework of corporate-dominated structures does not work. But neither is there any serious possibility, politically or economically, to transform those structures overnight. So each specific reform must, to use the language of Irving Howe, seek to unite the "near and the far," to make achievable gains that alter the rules of the game. To democratize economic decisions and tax policies is not simply to adopt two discrete and desirable goals; it is to move toward a shift in basic power relations.

The last great American Left did that, and it worked. The next American Left must be at least as audacious, which is to say, much more radical.

8

Justice Through
Justice

The very same changes that have made a new program a necessity for the next Left demand a new political strategy as well.

Fordism was not simply a way of organizing production. It created a powerful majority movement of social forces whose particular interests converged in the Fordist organization of the national economy. Moreover, it articulated a "public interest" so compelling that it came to dominate even those who originally opposed the whole project. When Richard Nixon said in 1971 that he was a "Keynesian," he was engaged in crass political opportunism designed to win him reelection the next year *and* was telling the truth. Similarly, President Giscard of France, having defeated the Socialists in 1974, proclaimed himself to be a "social democrat."

That unanimity collapsed along with Fordism itself. The conservative "wave" of the seventies and early eighties—the victory of the bourgeois coalition in Sweden and the turn to the right in Norway and Denmark, Margaret Thatcher, Ronald Reagan, and Helmut Kohl—was the result of the exhaustion of the Left as much as of anything else.

But now, the Left possibility is beginning to open up again. If that is going to lead to a next Left capable of creating a new model of economic growth through justice, there will have to be a political strategy that is as innovative as any of the programmatic changes proposed here. It will have to talk, not simply of "growth through justice," but of justice through justice, of the *moral* imperative of its program.

I

In his analysis of the French Revolution, Karl Marx came up with a concept that remains extremely useful to this day. In that epochal event, he said, the bourgeoisie's class interest in removing the feudal fetters that inhibited the development of a capitalist society coincided with the rational interest of every class in the society, which wanted to be rid of a decadent monarchy. Robespierre and his followers were not seen—and did not see themselves—as a "special interest" but as the representatives of the rights of all men and women. They led a "national class."

The young Marx thought that the nascent working class would rather rapidly become a huge majority of the society and therefore would quite naturally play the role of a national class. Moreover, he argued, the particular interest of the workers in ending capitalist exploitation was identical with the emancipatory interest of humanity as a whole. The workers, he said, would not, like the bourgeoisie, initiate the rule of a new elite based on a new form of exploitative property. They were the proponents of a social and democratic ownership that would seek to end exploitation itself.

Marx was wrong about some critical political questions in this analysis, as he himself later realized. In his *Theories of Surplus Value*, posthumously published and now read by only the most dedicated of Marxists, he recognized that capitalism was not evolving toward a simpler class structure, as he had assumed in his most popular single work, *The Communist Manifesto*. The intermediate strata were proliferating; there was the beginning of a new middle class as well as the persistence of the old.

Those trends accelerated after Marx's death, to the discomfort of his followers. How could socialism be brought about if the workers, and the conscious socialist workers in particular, were a minority? What should socialists do when they won not revolutionary power to create a totally new order, but some incremental influence over the existing order in a capitalist parliament? After World War I, when life posed that problem in Britain, Germany, and elsewhere, the Socialists, as we have seen, utterly failed to solve it.

In the United States the issue was not so clear-cut because of the absence of a mass socialist movement. But the broad Left of that period—the liberals, progressives, and populists, as well as the socialists—had to rally a political majority and to define the basis of their own legitimacy to govern. There already was, after all, a national class: business. Between 1896 and 1932, with the anomalous exception of the Wilson years, capital ruled quite openly in its own name. The business of the United States, Calvin Coolidge said in a brilliantly succinct phrase, is business. The evolution of capitalism itself had stymied the Left in the West—and not for the last time.

So it was that, in the thirties and forties, liberal Keynesianism in the United States and the socialist variant in Europe solved a political as well as an economic problem. If a certain socialization of mass consumption was seen as a practical necessity for the whole society, then the Left's demands for greater fairness and equality were no longer counterposed to economic growth and the well-being of the entire country but quintessential to it. The workers—understood in broadest compass as meaning all those nonowners suffering from a relative deprivation—were now a national class.

Thus, in the thirties, organizing drives in the United States and the great strikes in France won support from the middle class. Indeed, there was a kind of "Popular Front" culture that spread throughout the Western world, uniting all of the progressives behind antifascism, unionization, the Spanish Loyalists, peace, the struggle against racism, and all such good causes. There were books like *The Grapes of Wrath* and *Man's Hope*, songs of the international brigades in Spain and of textile workers in the United States. That Joseph Stalin and the world-wide movement he led were involved in all of this in sinister ways is another story. What is relevant here is that, once again, the Left seemed to stand for the highest hopes of all humanity in a time of struggle against fascism.

After World War II, the claims of the Left in Western society were less dramatic but politically even stronger. In Britain the Labour party pioneered in the creation—and naming—of the "welfare state," and the example spread throughout Europe. In the United States, the election of an Eisenhower gave a conservative legitimacy to the accomplishments of the New Deal. It was, after all, the Republican administration that created that quintessential Rooseveltian institution, the Department of Health and Welfare.

The climax of this political development took place, of course, in the sixties, i.e., simultaneously with the high point of the Great Prosperity. When John Kennedy announced, as he campaigned for tax cuts, that it was the citizen's patriotic duty to consume, the demands of the workers, of the poor, and the minorities were now seen as facilitating the happiness of all. Generosity was a stern imperative of political economy, not a wishy-washy sentiment of political idealists. Social justice and efficiency were, like the lambs and the lions of the biblical parable, going to lie down together.

The politics of the New Deal and its successor, liberalism, was based on a unity around economic issues. Franklin Roosevelt, it is important to remember, had refused to support any specific civil rights legislation—yet he moved black Americans into the Democratic party because his programs addressed their poverty. Indeed, in both Europe and the United States, Fordism was a "social class compromise." In return for certain basic organizing rights and a minimal standard of living, the workers and other oppositional strata renounced any intention of challenging the system as such.

But then in the 1950s, there was the first great social movement of the postwar era under the leadership of Martin Luther King Jr. Initially, it focused on noneconomic issues, like the right to vote and to obtain public accommodations without any racist restrictions. But by the mid-sixties, Dr. King and his movement had clearly understood that there was an economic, as well as a political, structure of racism. That was why King was campaigning for an economic and social bill of rights at the time of his death.

But this development put a political strain on the New Deal coalition, which had simply ignored the issue of race, political or economic. So did the emergence of a whole series of social movements that were not based primarily on economic demands, at least at the outset: the student activism of the sixties, the opposition to the war in Vietnam, the emergence of a new women's movement, the ecologists, the lesbians and gays. In each of these cases, the leadership of the movement was drawn from a growing stratum of the college-educated, the graduates of the mass higher-education system of the postwar period.

For class structure was undergoing a profound change. By the early eighties, a larger proportion of the labor force was engaged in professional and technical occupations (16 percent) than in work on the line in factories (12 percent). In a good many cases, the members of this new class were the children of the New Deal working class, but that did not keep them from adopting new attitudes. It was not just the economy that went through enormous change in the sixties; the culture shifted most perceptibly.

It is wrong to think that these social movements were independent of the economy. For as the blacks learned, followed by the feminists and the ecologists, social rights are half empty if they are not supported by corresponding economic rights. But that knowledge put further strains on a New Deal coalition based on loyalties developed during an era of greater class simplicity and interest. The economic success of Fordism led to social change that undermined the political basis of the whole development. And, not so incidentally, all of this came to a head precisely when Fordist economics went into crisis.

So it was that, in the seventies, American conservatives redefined the "national class." The workers and the poor, whose claims for justice in the sixties had been seen as a stimulus to affluence for all, were now accused of being a special interest.

The function of government was, it was argued, to stop "crowding out" the really creative people, the businessmen. It was the political function of supply-side economics to give a rationale for a preferential option for the entrepreneur. It was not, then, an accident that the Reagan tax act actually increased the taxes of the bottom 20 percent of the income structure while it cut the levies on the top 20 percent. Within the framework of the new conception of the national class, that made as much sense as the War on Poverty did in the sixties.

If the analysis of this book is right, that return to the values of Calvin Coolidge—for Reagan, too, could say that the business of America is business—is contradictory, crisis-prone and, in the second half of the eighties, about to unravel. But in a social and political setting that is much more complex than, and radically different from, that of the thirties, or even the sixties, what is the basis of a political strategy that could make the economic program of the last chapter a realistic possibility?

In what follows, I will write primarily of the United States. I assume that it is clear that I do not do so because I think that this country is a model of policy innovation. On the contrary, on many issues—like national health and children's allowances—it has lagged far behind the other advanced industrial democracies. I am especially aware of this whenever I travel to Canada. Here is a neighboring country with tremendous economic, social, and cultural similarities to the United States. Canadian baseball teams participate in the major leagues of our "national" sport. Yet when I talk to Canadian trade unionists, or activists from the New Democratic Party, I realize that ideas that are prophetic, marginal, or both in the United States are commonplaces in the mass democratic Left just north of our border.

In short, I feel our national inferiority on many policy issues, not its superiority. But I focus on the United States for two reasons. First, I know it best. Secondly, and of greater political and intellectual significance, this country is the decisive economic, political, and military power in the world for all the changes that have taken place. If it were to move to the left, that would have a dramatic and positive effect throughout the entire West and indeed around the globe. Franklin Roosevelt's improvised New

Deal was eventually of greater importance than Sweden's superior and theoretically articulated reforms. That is not fair. But it is a fact.

II

First of all, the next Left cannot assume that there is a spontaneous, homogeneous majority that need only become conscious of itself in order to play a central political role in Western society.

That was a basically Marxist assumption that permeated the thinking of American liberals as well as that of non-Marxist socialists on the Continent. It no longer applies. That is not to suggest for a moment that the working class has already disappeared or is about to do so. Even if one takes the most narrow of definitions—the workers are the blue-collar industrial proletariat—that is not true. As America enters the twenty-first century, there are still going to be millions of people toiling in factories, and they are likely to be better organized than those who are in offices and stores.

Clearly, those workers and their institutions are going to have to play a central role in the politics of the Left into the foreseeable future. And that is even more true if one expands the definition of the working class—and, much more to the point, if the unions manage to organizationally extend that definition—to the service sector, to include all those engaged in nonprofessional work at relatively low salaries or wages. What has changed is not that the working class has disappeared but that other strata have become much more important.

It is, of course, unclear—and politically up for grabs—as to what direction the new stratum of the college-educated from the postwar universities will take. They have been, it is well known, socially liberal and somewhat conservative on economics, but how they will react to the breakdown of the Reagan illusion is anyone's guess. But beyond that, these are times of new cleavages, not based on social class, and they must be taken into account.

Gender and race are now decisive categories, both in terms of

justice and political mobilization; women and minorities are the
most exploited and potentially the most dynamic people in society.

There is also the opposition between those in protected and
regular work and those in precarious occupations; between the
young and the old; between consumers with an interest in lower
prices and workers of all kinds with an interest in higher incomes; between cultural modernists and cultural traditionalists.

The political problem of the Left in the coming period is, I
believe, that of creating a program *and* a vision that can unite
very disparate social forces.

By far and large, the response of the American Democratic
party to the fracturing of its political base was to simply add on
new demands each time one of the emergent social forces crossed
a certain organizational threshold. At the San Francisco conven-
tion of the Democratic party in 1984, the platform was a sort of a
gigantic ideological smorgasbord, promising good things to a be-
wildering variety of constituencies. Almost every single plank
was indeed quite sound. What was missing was any sense of the
whole.

It is an intolerable irony that the "moderates" in the Democratic party—the Democratic Leadership Council under the
guidance of Charles Robb, former governor of Virginia, and
Bruce Babbitt, governor of Arizona—then began to work hard to
adopt a neo-Republican ideology even as the economic data of
1986 indicate that the crisis of Reaganism is not too distant. As
Daniel Patrick Moynihan, hardly a radical, put it in that year,
"By all means let us go on about self-reliance, gumption, and go-
gettingness. Nothing the matter with any of the above. But if
that is all there is to be by way of social policy, no one needs
Democrats. And if that is the social policy there is to be, Democrats shall have deserved their eclipse." To which it might
be added that, if the historic party of American liberalism abandons its own record and principles on the very eve of their renewed relevance, it would be an act of appalling political
stupidity.

Meanwhile, Ronald Reagan has managed to make business
the national class once again because he had successfully identified its interests with those of the nation as a whole—and, in-

deed, with the vision of the United States as a "city set upon a hill," an example for all who believe in freedom. According to his rationale, those who invest are the truly creative people, and government is in the business of frustrating their fine work for the common good. In outrageously playing favorites he was not, he reasoned, playing favorites, but helping everyone. And he counterposed himself to a Democratic party that was attacked as a warren of particular interests, unconcerned with the needs of the nation, determined only to add on another level of bureaucracy in order to pay off its client groups.

To counteract such half-truths and half-lies, the next Left must express its practical program in a language of sincere and genuine idealism. A politics without poetry will simply not be able to bring together all of the different, and sometimes antagonistic, forces essential to a new majority for a new program. The themes of that idealism have already been broached in terms of the specific concepts of the last chapter. Now I am more concerned with rhetoric—and philosophy.

The key concept of the next Left must be to achieve, not just growth, but new possibilities of individual and social life, and to do so through the stimulus of national and international social justice.

In arguing for various programs, I have taken great pains to stress their practical relevance and particularly their potential impact in promoting productivity. In part, that was a response to the Reagan-Thatcher, Western conservative view that more inequality is necessary to promote more efficiency. It is very important to document that the opposite is true. And I also stressed those pragmatic considerations because, contrary to its boasts, the Reagan administration did not begin to solve the crisis and, when that failure becomes apparent, the Left must have its response ready.

All those things must be said. But the Left must not hesitate in making a much larger point: that these necessities are also an opportunity, that their resolution will not simply enhance productivity, but will create the basis for a new way of living as well. The demands for an increase in free time as against working time, for a redefinition of the working life on the job through participation in decision making, and off the job through a qualitative increase in leisure time, are obvious examples.

In a significant number of cases in the United States, Canada, and Europe, as I have already shown, such changes are a matter of life and death for an incipient underclass that could be excluded from meaningful economic life and socially marginalized if present trends are allowed to operate unchecked. That is why the very concept of full employment presented in the last chapter was, to use the Swedish term, "solidaristic," i.e., aimed at doing the most for those with the least. In the United States and in Europe that means minorities and women.

But the other part of that formula is important, too: that such changes will radically improve the conditions of life of *everyone* in the society. The politics of *noblesse oblige* simply will not mobilize a majority that includes a very large number of people who are not poor yet are still suffering from relative deprivation. That is why the emphasis on the qualitative aspect of these proposals is so important.

Let me speak a bit out of my own experience. For the past fifteen years, I have been a professor at Queens College, a unit of the City University of New York—an institution that primarily teaches the sons and daughters of working people in a borough more noted for Edith and Archie Bunker than for its chic. Most of my students are absolutely determined to leave the working class or lower middle class into which they were born, and to make it into the great middle class, i.e., they are typically, even classically, American, even when they come from some of the new immigrant groups that abound in Queens.

But even though they are quite practical in their orientation—which means that most of them who take political science do so in order to get into law school, not to learn about the institutions of their country and the world—there is a very real idealism in their makeup that, in the seventies and eighties, has been deeply frustrated. Do not mistake me. They are not looking for a life of holy sacrifice and service. But, and this is a truth that the economic crisis has obscured, they also want to lead meaningful lives, to do fulfilling work. They do not aspire to be the best widget executives in history—even if difficult circumstances might force them to fall back on such a career.

As far as I can see, they are not that different from the youth of the sixties. The generational difference is not in their attitudes but in their possibilities. One of the reasons the young people of the Kennedy-Johnson years were attracted to the Peace Corps and Vista, to organizing for the civil rights and antiwar movements, or even to just dropping out for a while, is that the economy seemed affluent enough to permit them to experiment with their own lives. And the main reason that their younger brothers and sisters could not think in such terms in the seventies was that hard and uncertain times forced them to be "practical" in the narrowest sense of the word.

One of the aims of the Left economic program should be to allow people—particularly, but by no means exclusively, the young—more freedom to direct their own lives in a creative way. This is of enormous importance if, as I think is indeed the case, Fred Hirsch's *Social Limits of Growth* was a prophetic book. When, Hirsch argued, a very large number of people—let us say, the "baby boom" generation—attempts to follow the same individualistic path that was earlier trod by a much smaller minority, their ambition can become pathological.

There is already evidence accumulating that the new professional and technical stratum is not as privileged as it would like to be. When one-fifth of the labor force occupies that position at the end of the century, it will not be as exalted as it was in the fifties when it encompassed a mere 8 percent or so. For instance, an Urban Institute study has documented how a man passing from age forty to age fifty between 1953 and 1963 increased his earnings by 25 percent—but a forty-year-old in 1972 saw his real income drop 14 percent during the next decade. In 1949, it took 14 percent of the monthly income of a thirty-year-old to buy a median-priced house. In 1984, it took 44 percent of the median pay check.

So if the "baby boom" is not poor, neither is it as affluent as the generations that went before. That is frustrating for it and a waste for the society as well. If the immediate demand in this area is somewhat less than visionary—to adopt a target of the thirty-five-hour week—it should be presented within the context of a basic rethinking of the meaning of work in the society for college graduates as well as high school dropouts.

More broadly, there is a political correlation between these new ideas of the working life. There is a profound tradition in American life of "republicanism," of citizenship as a moral value and a basic commitment. Its historic source is, more often than not, to be found in Jefferson but, as Sean Wilentz has shown in his history of the early workers' movement, it permeated a good part of the society. In Nick Salvatore's fine biography of Eugene Victor Debs, he describes that spirit in a later period.

"The faith of Debs and his followers in the redemptive power of the ballot," Salvatore wrote, "is, from a current perspective, simply staggering. They took the republican tradition seriously and stressed the individual dignity and power inherent in the concept of citizenship. While frequently vague over exactly how to transform their society, these men and women had no doubt but that, if the people united, the vitality of that tradition would point the way." Jefferson had talked of the "little Republics," of the pervasive community involvement that was necessary if his concept of democracy was to prevail.

Can that tradition become more than nostalgic rhetoric? Was it a passing phase of a small-town America in which, as Robert Bellah and his coauthors of *Habits of the Heart* put it, "small-scale communities . . .were dominated by the classic citizens of a free republic, men of middling condition who shared similar economic and social conditions and whose ranks less affluent members of the population aspired to enter, often successfully"? Has that dream vanished in the reality of an urbanized mass society?

In a sense, the emphasis upon participation in the economy, which is so central to this analysis, is a call for creating those "small republics" in forms that Jefferson never imagined. And if that is going to work, it is not enough to have a legal right to participate in decisions, or even to have funds from the government to make that right effective. There must also be a different kind of spirit—not a Japanese spirit, with its roots in a kind of authoritarian paternalism that American business is so anxious to copy; but a democratic, and in some ways particularly American, spirit.

Preposterous? I think not. John Kennedy's inaugural was very much a cold-war document, and its idealism was, therefore, much too militant in its globalism. And yet it made a profound impact upon the United States—and helped to create a moral atmosphere in which experiments like the Peace Corps were possible—precisely because it appealed to that republican tradition and even to a notion with classical as well as French and Scottish roots, the idea of republican "virtue."

Ronald Reagan has brilliantly exploited the patriotism of war and national pride, and his success is a measure of a certain spiritual hunger that exists in the society—and, alas, can be partly satisfied by chauvinistic hokum. But I do not think that the Left can afford to leave the civic emotions to the Right. In a profound sense, that is our heritage more than theirs.

Secondly, the Left should hoist the rightist ideologues on their own petard, denouncing the scandalous waste and the contempt for productivity that is so often to be found in the upper reaches of managerial society.

The reactionary priorities of the Western Right have been based upon a commitment to productivity and entrepreneurship. But, as we have seen, the enormous handouts that have gone to the rich in the name of this goal have been wasted more often than not.

A very influential article in the *Harvard Business Review* in 1980 focused on this problem from a management-muckraking point of view. Robert H. Hayes and William J. Abernathy talked of, among many other things, the "pseudoprofessional" concept of the manager who could step into any company without any practical experience and, by using a technical and very short-term profit calculus, run the enterprise brilliantly. That technocratic ideology, Hayes and Abernathy concluded, was one of the reasons for the decline in productivity in the United States in the seventies.

Given these analyses, I suggest that the Left boldly and honestly turn the tables on the Right. For fifteen or so years the conservatives have claimed that stimulating the economy through short-run injustice will produce long-run justice. That is not simply immoral; it is also a demonstrable failure. There is in the United States, more than in any other Western country, an enormous amount of tax-subsidized corporate waste and speculation. The Left should propose to put those subsidies to work for useful and socially valuable purposes. And it should say that conservatism in managerial practice is, and long has been, a welfare-dependent traitor to its own entrepreneurial ideology.

Thirdly, it is critically important that all of this be done within an international perspective.

I have already pointed out that national Keynesianism simply does not work: not at all for the second-rank economies of the West, and only temporarily for the great exception, the United States. But there is also the enormous moral claim of the Third World and particularly of its most desperate people. That this claim has been regularly compromised by tyrants and demagogues is unquestioned; that the majority of the General Assembly of the United Nations has sometimes been wrong and mean is also true. But being victimized for several centuries is not an experience that necessarily creates generous and wise reactions.

And, no matter how some Third World politicians may have poorly served their own cause, their people should not be punished for their leaders' sins. Moreover, the extraordinary impact of the international television concert for African famine relief in 1985 should make it clear that there is a public that wants to be decent. That the Live Aid concert was a combination of media hype and music whose implicit values—hedonistic and even sadistic—often contradicted the explicit message of the event, is true enough. But so is the receptivity of masses of people that it revealed.

Again, that does not mean that the Left should propose that the affluent must philanthropically and self-righteously do something for "them." It certainly must not mean that the workers and poor people of the advanced countries should have their standards of living sacrificed in the name of an internationalism that is really a façade for the self-interest of multinational corporations. But it does mean that the economic relevance of a global

JUSTICE THROUGH JUSTICE • 193

recovery should also be stated in moral terms, as part of a commitment to the essential oneness of humanity.

And that, of course, relates to *the* central challenge of the last years of the twentieth century and the opening of the twenty-first: nuclear and conventional disarmament on a world scale. Here, the proposals of Willy Brandt should be put up front in the program of every Western party of the Left: that part of the savings from a disarmament process, which is utterly imperative in its own right, be used to end the agony of hunger and under-development in the Third World.

III

I want to end this book with a true parable.

In 1965, when Martin Luther King Jr. led thousands of marchers of different races and faiths and political persuasions through the empty streets of Montgomery, Alabama, the only spectators were the sullen and federalized national guardsmen, local people who had been forced to protect the lives of demonstrators they opposed. As a way of articulating the resentment of white, racist Montgomery, the city was everywhere decorated with Confederate flags.

When we reached the statehouse—the birthplace of the Confederacy itself—we could see only a single American flag in the distance. At that point some genius among the marchers led us in a revolutionary anthem: "The Star-Spangled Banner." We were dramatizing the fact that we represented the American tradition and not simply the claims of a black minority, that our cause was the cause of the entire society, not of an "interest group."

The democratic Left of Europe and North America must do the same, nationally and internationally. It is not just that its Fordist program of the past half-century no longer works and that it must go far beyond it. It will only be able to speak for the increasingly diverse peoples of the West if it rethinks and restates its own legitimacy.

What is needed in the late twentieth century is not just another program. What is needed is a restatement of the basic moral vision of the Western Left. For there is a sense in which Reaganomics is already in crisis—that its success *is* a crisis. For growth has brought persistent poverty, unemployment, homelessness, and hunger—and that has never happened before. The booby traps of the American economy will, I am convinced, explode sooner or later. But the next Left cannot content itself to sit around waiting for some catastrophe to save it from its own political impotence.

For if that next Left understands itself as a movement of genuine moral vision, then it can begin now, in the midst of a misshapen and outrageous "prosperity," to assemble the forces and develop the ideas of a new America in a new world.

Appendix

There are, as I noted at the outset, no footnotes in the text, and in what follows I will not list all of the books and articles that I used in writing this book. It is intended for an audience with an interest in public policy and a general education, and I see no need to include a detailed bibliography for specialists. There were, however, some books and sources that I used in depth, primarily as sources of concepts, and I want to acknowledge them, if only briefly.

The periodicals that I relied on throughout my work included *Dissent*, *Business Week*, the *New York Review of Books*, the *Economist*, the *Financial Times*, the *New Left Review*, *Le Monde*, *Libération*, *Le Nouvel Observateur*, *En Jeu*, *Die Neue Gesellschaft*, and *Die Neue Gesellschaft/Frankfurter Hefte*.

Some of the books that were most important to my analysis were:

Aglietta, Michel. *A Theory of Capitalist Regulation*. London: New Left Books, 1979 [1976].

Ambler, John S., ed. *The French Socialist Experiment*. Philadelphia: Institute for the Study of Human Issues, 1985.

Barrère, Christian, Gerard Kebadjian, and Olivier Weinstein. *Lire la crise*. Paris: PUF, 1983.

Beaud, Michel. *La politique économique de la gauche*. Vol. 1, *Le mirage de la croissance*. Paris: Syros, 1983. Vol. 2, *Le grand écart*. Paris: Syros, 1985.

Bernstein, Irving. *A History of the American Workers, 1920–1933*. Baltimore: Penguin, 1966.

Blackburn, Phil, Red Coombs, and Kenneth Greer. *Technology, Economic Growth and the Labor Process*. New York: St. Martin's, 1985.

Brody, David. *Workers in Industrial America*. New York: Oxford University Press, 1981.

Bucci-Glucksmann, Christine, and Goran Therborn. *Le défi social-démocrate*. Paris: Maspero, 1981.

Flannagan, Robert, David W. Soskice, and Lloyd Ulman. *Unions, Economic Stabilization and Incomes Policy: The European Experience*. Washington, D.C.: Brookings Institution, 1983.

Fonteneau, Alain, and Pierre Alain Muet. *La gauche face à la crise*. Paris: Presses de la fondation nationale des sciences politiques, 1985.

Harvey, David. *The Limits of Capital*. Chicago: University of Chicago Press, 1982.

Hayek, F. A. *The Constitution of Liberty*. Chicago: University of Chicago Press, 1960.

Kuttner, Robert. *The Economic Illusion*. Boston: Houghton Mifflin, 1985.

Lipietz, Alain. *L'audace ou l'enlisement*. Paris: Éditions de la découverte, 1984.

Meidner, Rudolf, and Anna Hedborg. *Modell Schweden*. Frankfurt: Campus Verlag, 1984.

Offe, Claus. *Contradictions of the Welfare State*. Edited by John Keane. Cambridge: MIT Press, 1984.

O'Connor, James. *Accumulation Crisis*. New York: Blackwell, 1984.

Piore, Michael, and Charles Sabel. *The Second Industrial Divide*. New York: Basic Books, 1984.

Robinson, Joan. *Economics: An Awkward Corner*. New York: Pantheon, 1967 [1966].

Rosanvallon, Pierre. *La crise de l'état-providence*. Paris: Seuil, 1981 [1983 ed].

Shaiken, Harley. *Work Transformed: Automation and Labor in the Computer Age*. New York: Holt, 1984.

Thurow, Lester. *The Zero Sum Solution*. New York: Simon and Schuster, 1985.

There were many other books and a large number of essays and articles that I consulted, a goodly number of them identified by author or title in the text itself. But the volumes listed above were most important for the conceptual framework of *The Next Left*. I am, of course, solely responsible for the use to which I put these analyses.